Annotated Legal Documents on Islam in Europe

Spain

Compiled, Annotated and Authored by

Juan Ferreiro
Jordi Moreras

BRILL

LEIDEN | BOSTON

The Library of Congress Cataloging-in-Publication Data is available online at http://catalog.loc.gov
LC record available at http://lccn.loc.gov/2021022037

Typeface for the Latin, Greek, and Cyrillic scripts: "Brill". See and download: brill.com/brill-typeface.

ISSN 2214-1340
ISBN 978-90-04-37827-8 (paperback)

This book is printed on acid-free paper and produced in a sustainable manner.

Annotated Legal Documents on Islam in Europe: Spain

Annotated Legal Documents on Islam in Europe

VOLUME 23

The titles published in this series are listed at *brill.com/ldie*

Contents

Foreword by the Editors

This is the twenty-third volume in the series *Annotated Legal Documents on Islam in Europe*. The publication of this series responds to the widespread lack of sound information about the legal status of Islam in Europe. In principle, this information is generally available to those who are willing to make the effort and know enough about the subject to ask the right questions of the digital search engines. But that requires both expertise and effort.

The series comes at an important historical juncture. Now the question looms large of how western-style legal systems are responding anew to a major religious group, Muslims, and their religion, Islam. This is not without historical precedent and yet the current environment is quite different and poses new challenges. Within either their European or overseas empires, some European legal systems had responded to Muslims as semi-autonomous communities with distinct legal status. In light of the inexorable movement in the direction of nation-states, including in those countries whose empires have dissolved, the basis of legal systems has changed dramatically and, everywhere, legal uniformity within secularised-Christian states became the order of the day. Minor exceptions have existed here and there for minorities, while broad human rights and freedoms were seen as adequate to accommodate minority groups, including religions.

European legal systems are now faced with a highly dynamic social and religious field, conditioned by continuing immigration from the contiguous Muslim-dominated world and elsewhere, and are poised between the question whether exceptional extensions of existing legal forms and instruments will be adequate to accommodate Muslims or whether greater, more systemic and structural changes will be required, or indeed demanded, by an increasing and more vocal Muslim population. Structural changes to long-held constitutional and legal values may also be at issue sooner or later.

A transnational Islamic field, the role of the influential Organisation of Islamic Cooperation, and the ever-present spectre of terrorism also play some role in this new insecure environment. Larger Muslim populations will also require that closer attention be paid to diversity and the variety of beliefs and practices that characterise Muslim life. Sectarian, regional, linguistic, political and intergenerational differences will become far more salient and have an interesting bearing upon, while posing complications for, wider societal and legal responses.

The principles characterising European legal systems, including human rights and freedoms and equal citizenship, may well not be considered adequate to accommodate Muslims. Muslims vary in their commitment to the values underpinning European legal systems and, often, they regard their religion and its practices as not liable to be encumbered by the demands of living in secular states the post-Reformation Christian character of which seems difficult for Muslims to access. Muslim practices may violate the basic principles of European legal systems, such as the equality of religion, gender and sexuality, the freedom of expression, or the right to marry. We are therefore already in a period of widespread conflict and resentment with uneasy, compromise legal solutions which may well be only temporary and liable to change frequently.

The aim of this series is to make this legislation available to both the interested researcher and the practising lawyer. Altogether the series is expected to comprise 32 volumes, one for each of the 27 countries of the European Union plus the United Kingdom, Norway and Switzerland, and a volume each dealing with the European Union (treaties, directives and decisions of the Court of Justice of the European Communities) and the European Court of Human Rights. Excerpts of relevant legislation are introduced and summarised by the volume compiler, and where court cases have provided significant interpretation of the law they will also be referred to. The legislation itself is reproduced in the original language, as the editors and the publisher agreed early on in the preparation of the series that any attempt to translate legislation into English would be unsatisfactory and risked being misleading. The comments and analysis by the compiler should give sufficient guidance to users to allow a decision whether to arrange a translation for their specific purposes.

Spain has gone through a period of major constitutional and legal re-orientation since the death of Franco in 1975, central to which was democratisation and a degree of distancing of the state from the Roman Catholic church. In principle a formal relationship with the state is now available through a status of corporate co-operation. Such an agreement was completed with the Islamic community in 1992 as well as with Jews and Protestants, while a new arrangement had earlier been reached with the Catholic church which separated the state and the church on the principle of the religious neutrality of the state. Smaller groups have the option of going for other less structured forms of recognition, and core religious freedoms apply even if no formal status has been obtained.

An attempt has been made to ensure that the volumes are structured in as similar a manner as possible. The starting point for this has been the thematic organisation used variously in the *Yearbook of Muslims in Europe* which Brill has published annually since 2009. But it has been only a starting point, and in each volume the compiler and the editors have agreed on the structure which makes most sense for the legislation of the country concerned. Normally one member of the editorial group takes responsibility for discussing the structure and compilation of each volume with the compiler: in this instance, this task was undertaken by Prof. Silvio Ferrari. We are also grateful to Kate Elliott for the care shown in copy editing the volume. The initiative for this project came from the publisher, where Nicolette van der Hoek and Nienke Brienen-Moolenaar have played an invaluable role in ensuring that the project has maintained its momentum. As editors, we appreciate how much their expertise contributes to ensuring that a project like this can run smoothly.

It is in the nature of such a project that each volume, if left as it stands, will gradually become out of date as new legislation and cases appear. From 2019 the series has become available online in a format which in due course will permit regular updating.

The Editors
April 2021

Abbreviations

AC	Cooperation Agreement
BOE	Spain's Official State Bulletin
CALR	Advisory Board for Religious Freedom
CC	Civil Code
CE	Spanish Constitution
CIE	Islamic Commission of Spain
FCJE	Federation of the Spanish Jewish Communities
FEERI	Spanish Federation of Islamic Religious Entities
FEREDE	Federation of Evangelical Religious Entities of Spain
LOE	Organic Law on Education
LOLR	Religious Freedom Act
RRE	Registry of Religious Entities
STC	Constitutional Court Sentence
UCIDE	Union of Islamic Communities of Spain

General Introduction

In the four decades since the approval of the Spanish Constitution (1978), which enshrines the principle of religious freedom (article 16), Spain has been defined as a non-denominational State. This meant abandoning the paradigm upheld by the previous political regime based on national Catholicism, which had allowed the Catholic Church to maintain privileged relations with respect to political power, and where any non-Catholic religious expression in the public space was controlled, and even persecuted. The religious freedom law of 1967, which recognised this freedom while making it compatible with the Catholic identity of the State, established a minimum tolerance towards other non-Catholic religious expressions, allowing their registration as confessional associations, which were not allowed to organise worship outside their places of worship without prior authorisation from the authorities.

Spanish society has become a democratic society, plural in the cultural sphere and also in the spiritual sphere,[1] and although the mono-denominational principle that was typical of the previous political regime is being overcome, many elements remain active that continue to relate Spanish society with Catholicism, based more on a link with tradition than on religious observance, and in which the State's institutional relations with the Spanish Episcopal Conference continue to have an impact in the Spanish political panorama.

Religious diversity has also acquired notable visibility in recent decades. An important part of this diversity is related to the settlement of immigrant groups, which have allowed the development of religious practices and rituals that did not have a previous social anchor. Another factor that has fuelled this diversity has been the revitalisation of religious traditions already present in Spanish society (as has been the case with the Protestant churches or Jehovah's Witnesses), which had earlier been kept discreetly in the background in a notoriously Catholic society.

Compared to other European realities, the Muslim presence in Spain presents a double peculiarity: on the one hand, the Muslim presence for more than seven centuries has left a remarkable cultural, artistic and linguistic legacy in Spanish society. On the other hand, more than five centuries later, in 1992, the Spanish State, by signing a Cooperation Agreement with Spanish Muslims,

1 See Díez de Velasco (2012) and the collection of monographs on religious diversity in the different Spanish regions, edited by the *Pluralism and Coexistence Foundation* of the Ministry of the Presidency (https://www.pluralismoyconvivencia.es/publicaciones/coleccion/coleccion-pluralismo-y-convivencia/, accessed: 14 November 2020).

established a legal framework for the recognition of Islam in Spain that would be the most advanced compared to other European countries with a greater Muslim presence.[2]

Islam, despite being one of the main religious traditions in the Spanish North African cities of Ceuta and Melilla, has been incorporated into Spanish society only since the early 1970s, first as a result of the first Muslim converts, and secondly as a result of the settlement of immigrant populations, mainly from the Maghreb, Sub-Saharan Africa, Pakistan and the Middle East. After half a century of contemporary presence of Islam in Spain a very heterogeneous group has formed, in which in addition to multiple nationalities and origins, a wide diversity of doctrinal tendencies and interpretations are manifest. Their inclusion in Spanish society, essentially marked in large part by their social condition as immigrants, has conditioned the social perceptions that have been elaborated around their integration. Various controversies and polemics have marked the trajectory of this presence, showing to a greater or lesser degree the sensibility of Spanish society with respect to Islam. Old stereotypes and prejudices in relation to Muslims are reactivated, updated and invoked in the face of controversies and tensions, especially in the case of the terrorist attacks in Europe, including on Spanish territory itself (as were the cases of Madrid on 11 March 2004, and Barcelona and Cambrils on 17 August 2017).

The pandemic caused by covid-19 has had a global impact on Spanish society, as well as on the different religious communities that are part of it. In the specific case of Islam, the death in April 2020 of Riay Tatary, a historic Spanish Muslim leader and president of the Islamic Commission of Spain (CIE), has begun a new period for the representative entity of Islam. In July 2020, a new CIE board of directors was elected, chaired by Dr. Ayman Adlbi, a 74-year-old doctor of Syrian origin.

In this framework of complex relationships, the incorporation of Islam as a religious tradition and of Muslims as a social collective is conditioned by the articulation of a broad legal framework relating to a presence that can no longer be understood as an alien reality in Spanish society, even though it continues to be questioned by some social discourses. The paradox arises that while the first generation of Muslims born into Spanish society is emerging, Islamophobic arguments are growing in line with the social and political environment in Europe.

This work aims to define this framework of legal articulation of the recognition of Islam in Spain, based on the analysis of the legal and institutional

---

2 See Moreras (2002).

instruments that have been put in place in recent decades in relation to the Islamic singularity. Along with this analysis, we will incorporate some sociological elements of context, better to understand this context of legal and institutional recognition.

CHAPTER 1

Status of Religious Communities

1.1 General and Specific Principles

1.1.1 *Religious Freedom*

In general terms, relations between public authorities and religious denominations should be developed while respecting general principles of both religious freedom and equality. The Spanish Constitution (CE) proclaims in its preliminary part, right after the Preamble, that Freedom and Equality are two of the fundamental values of the legal system.

Constitución Española de 1978
BOE, 311, 29 de diciembre de 1978.

Título Preliminar

Artículo 1.1: España se constituye en un Estado social y democrático de Derecho, que propugna como valores superiores de su ordenamiento jurídico la libertad, la justicia, la igualdad y el pluralismo político.

Furthermore, chapter II (Rights and Liberties), under Part I (Fundamental Rights and Duties), proclaims as fundamental rights equality (art. 14) and religious and ideological freedom. The only prescribed limits of religious freedom (whether of individuals or groups) are those necessary for the maintenance of public order, which is protected by the law (art. 16.1).

Título I De los derechos y deberes fundamentales

Capítulo 2: Derechos y libertades

Sección 1.ª De los derechos fundamentales y de las libertades públicas

Artículo 14: Los españoles son iguales ante la ley, sin que pueda prevalecer discriminación alguna por razón de nacimiento, raza, sexo, religión, opinión o cualquier otra condición o circunstancia personal o social.

Artículo 16.1: Se garantiza la libertad ideológica, religiosa y de culto de los individuos y las comunidades sin más limitación, en sus manifestaciones, que la necesaria para el mantenimiento del orden público protegido por la ley.

Organic Law 7/1980 of 5 July on Religious Freedom (or the Religious Freedom Act, LOLR) implements this fundamental right proclaimed in the Constitution. This law refers in its article 2 to several manifestations of religious freedom of individuals and communities.

Ley Orgánica 7/1980, de 5 de julio, de Libertad Religiosa.
BOE núm. 177, de 24 de julio de 1980

Artículo 2:
1. La libertad religiosa y de culto garantizada por la Constitución comprende, con la consiguiente inmunidad de coacción, el derecho de toda persona a: a) Profesar las creencias religiosas que libremente elija o no profesar ninguna; cambiar de confesión o abandonar la que tenía; manifestar libremente sus propias creencias religiosas o la ausencia de las mismas, o abstenerse de declarar sobre ellas. b) Practicar los actos de culto y recibir asistencia religiosa de su propia confesión; conmemorar sus festividades, celebrar sus ritos matrimoniales; recibir sepultura digna, sin discriminación por motivos religiosos, y no ser obligado a practicar actos de culto o a recibir asistencia religiosa contraria a sus convicciones personales. c) Recibir e impartir enseñanza e información religiosa de toda índole, ya sea oralmente, por escrito o por cualquier otro procedimiento; elegir para sí, y para los menores no emancipados e incapacitados, bajo su dependencia, dentro y fuera del ámbito escolar, la educación religiosa y moral que esté de acuerdo con sus propias convicciones. d) Reunirse o manifestarse públicamente con fines religiosos y asociarse para desarrollar comunitariamente sus actividades religiosas de conformidad con el ordenamiento jurídico general y lo establecido en la presente Ley Orgánica.
2. Asimismo, comprende el derecho de las Iglesias, Confesiones y Comunidades religiosas a establecer lugares de culto o de reunión con fines religiosos, a designar y formar a sus ministros, a divulgar y propagar su propio credo, y a mantener relaciones con sus propias organizaciones o con otras confesiones religiosas, sea en territorio nacional o en el extranjero.
3. Para la aplicación real y efectiva de estos derechos, los poderes públicos adoptarán las medidas necesarias para facilitar la asistencia religiosa en

> los establecimientos públicos, militares, hospitalarios, asistenciales, penitenciarios y otros bajo su dependencia, así como la formación religiosa en centros docentes públicos.

Given that there are no unlimited fundamental rights, article 3 of this law refers to two kinds of limits to religious freedom: fundamental rights of others and public order. The same law describes public order as a three-dimensional concept which includes public security, public health and public morality.

> Artículo 3.
> 1. El ejercicio de los derechos dimanantes de la libertad religiosa y de culto tiene como único límite la protección del derecho de los demás al ejercicio de sus libertades públicas y derechos fundamentales, así como la salvaguardia de la seguridad, de la salud y de la moralidad pública, elementos constitutivos del orden público protegido por la Ley en el ámbito de una sociedad democrática.

Religious freedom is normally understood as a fundamental right. But it can also be accepted as a tenet: as a constitutive part of Church-State relations. As a fundamental right, this freedom belongs only to individuals and communities, the only holders of this fundamental right. Also, as a fundamental right, religious freedom must also be guaranteed by the State, based on religious neutrality that leads to religious pluralism.

1.1.2 *Religious Equality*

Equality, apart from being proclaimed as a principle in art. 9.2 of the Spanish Constitution, is also underlined as a fundamental right enshrined in art. 14 which proclaims the equality of all Spaniards before the law and prohibits discrimination, especially on the basis of "birth, race, sex, religion, and opinion or any other condition or personal or social circumstance".

Equality is not uniformity. Equality is giving each their due; in other words, treating equals as equals and unequally those who are not. On the other hand, uniformity is giving everyone the same thing regardless of their circumstances. In accordance with equality, public powers (Government, Judges or Legislators) can establish differences, if those differences are reasonable, justified and proportional with the goal they seek. Otherwise, they would be discriminatory.

The Spanish Constitution establishes a particular model of relationship between the State and religions. After recognising religious freedom for individuals and communities (16.1) and prohibiting forced declarations of personal beliefs (16.2), article 16.3 refers to two specific principles, namely the principle of separation between State and denominations and the principle of cooperation, which have a natural tendency to contradict each other, but are forced to live together.

> Constitución Española de 1978
>
> Artículo 9.2: Corresponde a los poderes públicos promover las condiciones para que la libertad y la igualdad del individuo y de los grupos en que se integra sean reales y efectivas; remover los obstáculos que impidan o dificulten su plenitud y facilitar la participación de todos los ciudadanos en la vida política, económica, cultural y social.
>
> Artículo 16.2: Nadie podrá ser obligado a declarar sobre su ideología, religión o creencias.
>
> Artículo 16.3: Ninguna confesión tendrá carácter estatal. Los poderes públicos tendrán en cuenta las creencias religiosas de la sociedad española y mantendrán las consiguientes relaciones de cooperación con la Iglesia Católica y las demás confesiones.

1.1.3 *Non-religious State* (*Separation & Neutrality*) *and Cooperation*

CE article 16.3 establishes that "no religion shall have a State character". The formula used in the Constitutional draft was more convincing: "the State is non-religious". However, that expression did not survive the drafting. Maybe because it was too similar to the expression used in the Constitution of 1932 in the Second Spanish Republic: "the State has no official religion".[1]

The formula adopted in the current Constitution of 1978 limits its scope to recognising the secular character of the State for two reasons. In the first place, this affirmation should be proclaimed in the preliminary part of the Constitution, where the State defines its essential character. But instead, it has been proclaimed under "Title I" regarding Fundamental Rights (art. 16.3). Second, it is a timid expression because the subject of the sentence is not "the State" (as it should be) but denominations ("no religion"). So, the sentence focuses directly on denominations (they do not have State character) and only in an indirect way on the State. And, supposedly, this expression refers to the attitude that the State must adopt towards religions. Nonetheless, the constitutional expression

1 See J. Ferreiro (2005), *Relaciones Iglesia-Estado en la II República Española* Barcelona: Ediciones Atelier.

("No religion shall have a State character") displays the two concepts or pillars sustaining the non-religious State principle: separation between Church and State and the neutrality of public institutions in religious affairs.

1.1.3.1 Separation

The basic idea of this principle is that religions remain independent and autonomous in relation to public institutions (central government, autonomous regions and municipalities). Public institutions cannot interfere in the sphere of churches and denominations, which should organise themselves freely. By contrast, religions cannot interfere in the realm of the State. Thus, denominations cannot demand that their doctrine regarding any issue (abortion, marriage, etc.) become effective law.

Only Parliament (or any other institution with legislative competence) can approve laws, considering the demands and needs of the different social sectors, but without necessarily becoming a transmission belt for a certain ideology or religious belief. According to the standards of separation, a religious leader cannot become a public official by reason of his religious status. If a priest, pastor, rabbi or imam wants to become a public worker he must, like any citizen, pass public examinations, inspired by the constitutional principles of equality, merit and ability.

The principle of non-intervention of representatives of religious traditions in social and political matters (within the framework of the principle of separation) should not be confused with freedom of expression. Criticism of a law, government policy or judicial decision pronounced by a cleric or a religious denomination must be understood as a manifestation of freedom of expression, and not as a desire to interfere in the sphere of the State. If politicians do not like the opinion of any church about their decisions or actions, they can counter that judgment by also exercising freedom of expression.

1.1.3.2 Neutrality

The State is neutral on religious issues. That implies the obligation, not only not to adopt any religion, but also not to evaluate any type of religious expression or the content of beliefs. Embracing, rejecting or criticising a denomination is the right only of citizens and communities, which are those who have the right to religious freedom. The State has no competence in relation to any manifestation of faith and, therefore, cannot assess its legitimacy or establish preferences among the religious beliefs of the citizens.[2]

2 "The articulation of a register ... does not habilitate the State to undertake an activity of con-

In this way the State can neither establish an official religion nor declare itself atheist or secularist or express any kind of prejudice with respect to religion. A biased State maintains prejudices against religious beliefs, and therefore treats them worse than other associations (cultural, social, sports …). Differences in treatment due to religious nature are examples of discrimination.

According to the principle of neutrality, the term "cult" is not accepted as a legal term, due to its negative connotations (implying a false religion or belief). According to a secular (neutral) legal language, the State must accept that religious communities are those that are considered by themselves as such, and also those that have decided to register in the Registry of Religious Entities (RRE) of the Ministry of Justice (since February of 2020 under the Ministry of the Presidency).[3]

But neutrality does not mean that the State must accept any religious denomination. Not only must groups that wish to be recognised as religions demonstrate that their purposes lie within the realm of spirituality and belief, but, like any other type of association, they must not exceed the legal limits established in the Constitution. Any group that pursues objectives or uses means classified as criminal will be considered illegal (article 22.2 of the Constitution).

Constitución Española de 1978

Artículo 22
1. Se reconoce el derecho de asociación.
2. Las asociaciones que persigan fines o utilicen medios tipificados como delito son ilegales. […]

---

trol to determine the legitimacy of religious beliefs … but only to verify, deriving to that end a mere act of stating and not rating, that the applicant group is not one of those entities excluded by article 3.2 of the LOLR, and that the activities and behaviours developed for its practice do not threaten the rights of others in the exercise of their fundamental freedoms and rights, nor do they threaten the security, health and morality of the public, as elements that enshrine the public order protected by the law in a democratic society, which are referred to in CE article 16.1" (Constitutional Court STC 46/2001).

3 Decree 373/2020, of 18 February, which develops the basic organic structure of the Ministry of the Presidency, Relations with the Courts and Democratic Memory, article 7: 1. It corresponds to the Under-secretariat of the Presidency, Relations with the Courts and Democratic Memory … q) Ordinary relations with religious entities; r) The elaboration of the proposals of agreements and cooperation agreements with the churches, confessions and religious communities and, in their subsequent follow-up; s) The direction and management of the Registry of Religious Entities, the ordering of the exercise of its function and the proposed resolution of the administrative appeals that are filed against the acts derived from the exercise of this registry function.

But in addition, the Religious Freedom Act establishes that the exercise of religious freedom has two limitations: the fundamental right of other people, and public order (in terms of security, health and public morality).[4]

The Constitutional Court has frequently stressed that these limits should be based not on mere presumptions but on facts, for example, whether a religious group has been convicted by a final judgment or by any kind of judgment.[5] If the RRE detects indications or insinuations (not just hard evidence) that suggest that the group requesting registration is carrying out illegal activities against fundamental rights or public order, following the general Law on associations it should send the request file with all the documents in it either to the prosecutor or to the Judges in order to initiate the relevant procedure.[6]

> Ley Orgánica 1/2002, de 22 de marzo, reguladora del Derecho de Asociación
> «BOE» núm. 73, de 26/03/2002.
>
> Artículo 30. Régimen jurídico de la inscripción.
> [...]
> 4. Cuando se encuentren indicios racionales de ilicitud penal en la constitución de la entidad asociativa, por el órgano competente se dictará resolución motivada, dándose traslado de toda la documentación al Ministerio Fiscal o al órgano jurisdiccional competente, y comunicando esta circunstancia a la entidad interesada, quedando suspendido el procedimiento administrativo hasta tanto recaiga resolución judicial firme.

In summary, the main consequence of secularism that derives from this dimension of neutrality is that the State cannot assume any religious principle as a parameter for measuring the legitimacy or illegitimacy of its performance. Unlike what was established during the Franco regime, the State does not obtain its legitimacy from any divine mandate.

---

4 See chapter 1.1.1.

5 As the Constitutional Court declared, "only when the existence of a certain danger against the public security, health and morality as they should be recognised in a democratic society has been accredited before the court, is it pertinent to invoke public order as a limit to the exercise of the right to religious freedom and freedom of worship" (FJ11).

6 See Pelayo (2007: 313).

1.1.3.3 Cooperation

The principle of cooperation is reflected in article 16.3 of the Spanish Constitution,[7] which orders public authorities to do two specific things: consider the religious beliefs of the Spanish population and maintain the resulting relations of cooperation with the Catholic Church and all other denominations.

From this double mandate it is possible to extract certain consequences. In the first place, in that article the concept of cooperation refers just to religious faiths. Although the State can obviously cooperate with non-religious ideological groups, article 16.3 of CE refers to the cooperation of public authorities with the Catholic Church (specifically mentioned) and other religious denominations. Secondly, relations of cooperation imply the existence of the State and religions as two independent and autonomous entities. In other words, cooperation ratifies the principle of separation. Thirdly, cooperation implies a positive view of the religious phenomenon. Denominations are considered to be potentially positive; otherwise, the Constitution would not order the public powers to cooperate with them. Finally, in line with the principle of freedom, cooperation should take place only at the request of denominations, because some denominations might prefer not to have any contact with the State.

The Spanish Constitution does not mention any specific method of cooperation. But on 3 January 1979, five days after the Constitution came into force, the Spanish State signed an International Treaty with the Holy See. Indirectly, by this decision the State was exhibiting a political method of cooperation, which a year later in the Religious Freedom Act 1980 was also offered to other denominations, but with some nuances. According to article 7.1 of this Law the State, "considering the existing religious beliefs in Spanish society", may be able to establish Cooperation Agreements "with the Registered Denominations which by their context and number of followers have reached a deeply rooted status in Spain". The Treaty with the Holy See incorporates a section related to the economic contribution by the Spanish State to the maintenance of the activities of the Catholic Church. The format of this funding has changed over time, but it is substantially different from the state's financial contributions to recognised confessions and to those with a cooperation agreement (see 2.2).

In other words, denominations that want to opt for a cooperation agreement should fulfil these three conditions:

a. Be registered in the RRE, nowadays under the Ministry of Presidency.
b. Obtain "deeply rooted" (*notorio arraigo*) character in Spanish society.

7 See chapter 1.1.2.

To clarify this new legal concept ("deeply rooted" status or "attested rootedness"), the Religious Freedom Act offered only two criteria: context and the number of believers. According to scientific and administrative doctrine, the word "context" referred not only to a significant number of followers spread throughout the whole or part of Spanish territory, but also to different features such as the historical presence of the applicant denomination in the country, the importance of its social, altruistic and cultural activities, the number of places of worship, the number of ministers of worship in proportion to its members etc.[8]

> Ley Orgánica 7/1980, de 5 de julio, de Libertad Religiosa.
>
> Artículo 7.
> 1. El Estado, teniendo en cuenta las creencias religiosas existentes en la sociedad española, establecerá, en su caso, Acuerdos o Convenios de cooperación con las Iglesias, Confesiones y Comunidades religiosas inscritas en el Registro que por su ámbito y número de creyentes hayan alcanzado notorio arraigo en España. En todo caso, estos Acuerdos se aprobarán por Ley de las Cortes Generales.
> 2. En los Acuerdos o Convenios, y respetando siempre el principio de igualdad, se podrá extender a dichas Iglesias, Confesiones y Comunidades los beneficios fiscales previstos en el ordenamiento jurídico general para las Entidades sin fin de lucro y demás de carácter benéfico.

Due to this legal imprecision, for many years the institution which "de facto" granted bodies the status of a deeply rooted denomination was the Advisory Board for Religious Freedom (CALR), a consultative body appointed by the Ministry of the Presidency, whose task, according to the LOLR, is to prepare reports and proposals on issues linked with religious freedom, and particularly to prepare the mandatory report before the signing of the Cooperation Agreement.

> Ley Orgánica 7/1980, de 5 de julio, de Libertad Religiosa.
>
> Artículo ocho.
> Se crea en el Ministerio de Justicia una Comisión Asesora de Libertad Religiosa compuesta de forma paritaria y con carácter estable por representantes de la Administración del Estado, de las Iglesias, Confesiones o

8 See Fernández-Coronado (1995: 45–47).

Comunidades religiosas o Federaciones de estas, en las que, en todo caso, estarán las que tengan arraigo notorio en España, y por personas de reconocida competencia, cuyo asesoramiento se considere de interés en las materias relacionadas con la presente Ley. En el seno de esta Comisión podrá existir una Comisión Permanente, que tendrá también composición paritaria.
A dicha Comisión corresponderán las funciones de estudio, informe y propuesta de todas las cuestiones relativas a la aplicación de esta Ley, y particularmente, y con carácter preceptivo, en la preparación y dictamen de los Acuerdos o Convenios de cooperación a que se refiere el artículo anterior.

This article was implemented by Royal Decree 932/2013, of 29 November, regulating the Advisory Commission on Religious Liberty.

Real Decreto 932/2013, de 29 de noviembre, por el que se regula la Comisión Asesora de Libertad Religiosa
BOE núm. 300, de 16 de diciembre de 2013

Artículo 2. Naturaleza y fines de la Comisión.
1. La Comisión Asesora de Libertad Religiosa es el órgano consultivo del Gobierno en materia de libertad religiosa.
2. La Comisión podrá asimismo asesorar a las Administraciones Públicas en relación con la aplicación tanto de la Ley Orgánica de Libertad Religiosa, como de los Acuerdos celebrados por parte del Estado español con las confesiones religiosas, sin perjuicio de las competencias que la normativa vigente atribuya en la materia a otros órganos.
3. La Comisión es un órgano colegiado de los previstos en el artículo 22.2 de la Ley 30/1992, de 26 de noviembre, de Régimen Jurídico de las Administraciones Públicas y del Procedimiento Administrativo Común, y en el artículo 40.1 de la Ley 6/1997, de 14 de abril, de Organización y Funcionamiento de la Administración General del Estado, adscrito orgánica y funcionalmente al Ministerio de Justicia, a través de la Dirección General de Cooperación Jurídica Internacional y Relaciones con las Confesiones.
4. La Comisión tiene por objeto el estudio, seguimiento, informe y la realización de propuestas de todas aquellas materias relacionadas con el desarrollo, impulso y promoción efectiva del derecho de libertad religiosa.
Artículo 3. Funciones de la Comisión.
Para el cumplimiento de los fines establecidos en el artículo anterior, la Comisión tendrá las funciones siguientes:

a) Conocer e informar preceptivamente los proyectos de acuerdos o convenios de cooperación a que se refiere el artículo 7 de la Ley Orgánica 7/1980, de 5 de julio.
b) Conocer e informar los proyectos de disposiciones de carácter general que afecten a la aplicación de la Ley Orgánica 7/1980, de 5 de julio.
c) Conocer e informar los proyectos de disposiciones de carácter general que afecten a la aplicación y desarrollo de los acuerdos celebrados entre el Estado español y las confesiones religiosas.
d) Conocer e informar los anteproyectos de ley y cualesquiera otras disposiciones generales de la Administración General del Estado que regulen materias concernientes al derecho de libertad religiosa.
e) Emitir informe sobre la declaración de notorio arraigo de las iglesias, confesiones o federaciones de las mismas.
f) Emitir informe de las cuestiones relacionadas con la inscripción y cancelación de las entidades religiosas, que le sean sometidas a su consulta.
g) Emitir informes sobre las normas que incidan en el ejercicio del derecho de libertad religiosa que hayan sido dictadas por las Comunidades Autónomas, que el Gobierno, a través del Ministro de Justicia, someta a su consulta.
h) Emitir informes sobre los asuntos concernientes a su ámbito de competencias que el Gobierno, a través del Ministro de Justicia, someta a su consideración.
i) Estudiar y presentar propuestas al Gobierno de cuantas medidas considere oportunas en el ámbito de la libertad religiosa, sin perjuicio de las competencias que la normativa vigente atribuya en la materia a otros órganos.
j) Elaborar y elevar anualmente un informe al Gobierno sobre la situación del derecho de libertad religiosa en España.
k) Recabar información sobre actuaciones de las Administraciones Públicas relacionadas con el desarrollo y ejercicio del derecho de libertad religiosa.
l) Cualquier otra función que, en el ámbito de sus competencias, se le atribuya por alguna disposición legal o reglamentaria.

Nowadays Royal Decree 593/2015[9] defines "deeply rooted character", so adding an important attempt to clarify the imprecision of that concept.

9 Royal Decree 593/2015, of July 3, which regulates the declaration of well-established roots of religious confessions in Spain.

Real Decreto 593/2015, de 3 de julio, por el que se regula la declaración de notorio arraigo de las confesiones religiosas en España
BOE» núm. 183, de 1 de agosto de 2015

Capítulo II Procedimiento para la declaración de notorio arraigo en España

Artículo 3. Requisitos.
Para la declaración de notorio arraigo en España a que se refiere el artículo 7.1 de la Ley Orgánica 7/1980, de 5 de julio, las iglesias, confesiones o comunidades religiosas deberán reunir los requisitos siguientes:
a) Llevar inscritas en el Registro de Entidades Religiosas treinta años, salvo que la entidad acredite un reconocimiento en el extranjero de, al menos, sesenta años de antigüedad y lleve inscrita en el citado Registro durante un periodo de quince años.
b) Acreditar su presencia en, al menos, diez comunidades autónomas y/o ciudades de Ceuta y Melilla.
c) Tener 100 inscripciones o anotaciones en el Registro de Entidades Religiosas, entre entes inscribibles y lugares de culto, o un número inferior cuando se trate de entidades o lugares de culto de especial relevancia por su actividad y número de miembros.
d) Contar con una estructura y representación adecuada y suficiente para su organización a los efectos de la declaración de notorio arraigo.
e) Acreditar su presencia y participación activa en la sociedad española.

c. As established in the Religious Freedom Act (art. 7), the Cooperation Agreements must be passed as Laws in the Parliament.

In 1992, twelve years after the Religious Freedom Act came into force, the State signed three Cooperation Agreements with the representative bodies of the three religious groups that by that time had obtained the status of deeply rooted religions: the Islamic Commission of Spain (CIE), the Federation of Evangelical Religious Entities of Spain (FEREDE) and the Federation of the Spanish Jewish Communities (FCJE).

These cooperation agreements, as established in article 7 of the LOLR, were passed in the Parliament as Laws 24, 25 and 26 of 10 November 1992,[10] dealing

10 Ley 26/1992, de 10 de noviembre, por la que se aprueba el Acuerdo de Cooperación del Estado con la Comisión Islámica de España. BOE núm. 272, de 12/11/1992. Ley 26/1992, de 10 de noviembre, por la que se aprueba el Acuerdo de Cooperación del Estado con la Federación de Entidades Evangélicas de España. BOE núm. 272, de 12/11/1992. Ley 26/1992, de

with issues such as the legal protection of places of worship, the legal status of ministers of worship and their inclusion in the Social Security System, the civil effects of marriages celebrated according to Jewish, Evangelical and Muslim rites, religious chaplaincy in public establishments, religious education in public schools, and tax benefits applied to specific goods and activities belonging to the FEREDE,[11] the CIE[12] and the FCJE[13] as signatories to the Agreement.

The mention in the Constitution of the Catholic Church has never been without controversy in the Constituent Assembly's debates. For some deputies, this was evidence that a kind of covert religious State was being proposed that contradicted the principle of secularisation of the State. For others, it showed only a mere recognition of the influence of the Catholic Church in the history of Spain. However, at the end of the debates, this mention prevailed. Even if mentioning the Catholic Church in the Constitution was a legally questionable issue, it was reasonable from a political point of view, because the goal at that moment (1978: the period of Spanish political transition) was that transition from a religious State (the previous dictatorial regime) to a non-denominational (or secular) State could be accomplished in a soft and non-traumatic way.

The Spanish model of State-Church relations is maintained in a combination between the principle of a non-religious State and the principle of cooperation. It is what makes Spanish secularism different from the French *laïcité* model: denominations are considered as a legal concept (not defined by the State, however) and public powers must cooperate with them if cooperation is required.

1.2 Four Types of Legal Recognition

From a legal perspective we can distinguish between four types of legal recognition: legal terms, which have been adopted by the different denominations in Spain:

10 de noviembre, por la que se aprueba el Acuerdo de Cooperación del Estado con la Federación de Comunidades Israelitas de España. BOE núm. 272, de 12/11/1992.

11 Federación de Entidades Religiosas Evangélicas de España http://www.ferede.es/.

12 Comisión Islámica de España http://comisionislamicadeespana.org/.

13 Federación de Comunidades Judías de España http://www.fcje.org/.

1.2.1 *Non-registered Religious Entities*

Religious entities need not register to be entitled to religious freedom. Section 16 of the Constitution, as we have seen,[14] guarantees the fundamental right of religious freedom to all religious communities, whatever legal form they adopt, if they respect the fundamental rights of others and public order. This fundamental right cannot depend on the act of being registered in a public register.

Registering in the Register of Religious Entities (RRE) is one way in which a religious group may become a religious legal entity. Another possibility is becoming an association under the Law of Associations. In this case, the requirements are the submission by at least three individuals of an agreement to become an association and the presentation of bylaws (in a public or private document) approving the organisation and functioning of the association.

Ley Orgánica 1/2002, de 22 de marzo reguladora del Derecho de Asociación
BOE» núm. 73, de 26 de marzo de 2002

Capítulo II: Constitución de las asociaciones

Artículo 5 Acuerdo de constitución: 1. Las asociaciones se constituyen mediante acuerdo de tres o más personas físicas o jurídicas legalmente constituidas, que se comprometen a poner en común conocimientos, medios y actividades para conseguir unas finalidades lícitas, comunes, de interés general o particular, y se dotan de los Estatutos que rigen el funcionamiento de la asociación. 2. El acuerdo de constitución, que incluirá la aprobación de los Estatutos, habrá de formalizarse mediante acta fundacional, en documento público o privado. Con el otorgamiento del acta adquirirá la asociación su personalidad jurídica y la plena capacidad de obrar, sin perjuicio de la necesidad de su inscripción a los efectos del artículo 10. 3. Lo establecido en este artículo se aplicará también para la constitución de federaciones, confederaciones y uniones de asociaciones.

Another legal possibility for a denomination that does not want to be registered as a denomination is to act in the legal form of a foundation.[15]

---

14 See chapter 1.1.1.
15 Law 50/2002, of 23 December, of Foundations.

Ley 50/2002, de 26 de diciembre, de Fundaciones.
BOE núm. 310, de 27 de diciembre de 2002

Artículo 2. Concepto. 1. Son fundaciones las organizaciones constituidas sin fin de lucro que, por voluntad de sus creadores, tienen afectado de modo duradero su patrimonio a la realización de fines de interés general. 2. Las fundaciones se rigen por la voluntad del fundador, por sus Estatutos y, en todo caso, por la Ley.
Artículo 4. Personalidad jurídica. 1. Las fundaciones tendrán personalidad jurídica desde la inscripción de la escritura pública de su constitución en el correspondiente Registro de Fundaciones. La inscripción sólo podrá ser denegada cuando dicha escritura no se ajuste a las prescripciones de la ley.
Artículo 10. Inscripción en el Registro.
1. Las asociaciones reguladas en la presente Ley deberán inscribirse en el correspondiente Registro, a los solos efectos de publicidad.

In either of those cases, such denominations can enrol in the relevant register: if they have adopted the form of a legal foundation in the National Register of Foundations (Ministry of Justice) or, if they have adopted the form of an association, in the National Registry of Associations, under the Ministry of Interior (if their area of activity is the whole country) or in any of the registers of associations existing in each of the 17 Autonomous Communities (regions) in Spain if they conduct their acts of worship in only one of those Autonomous Regions.

Nevertheless, if any denomination decides not to register as a denomination either in the RRE (Ministry of Presidency) or as a legal association or foundation in its respective register, this shall not affect its entitlement to the fundamental right of religious freedom. This is the case of some Islamic groups that did not want to appear in any public register.

1.2.2 *Religious Entities Enrolled in the Register of Religious Entities*

As suggested in the law of associations and also prescribed in the Religious Freedom Act, denominations have the option to enrol in a special nationwide register: the Register of Religious Entities (RRE), which is under the jurisdiction of the Ministry of Presidency.

Ley Orgánica 1/2002, de 22 de marzo reguladora del Derecho de Asociación

Artículo 1. Objeto y ámbito de aplicación.
[…]
3. Se regirán por su legislación específica los partidos políticos; los sindicatos y las organizaciones empresariales; las iglesias, confesiones y comunidades religiosas; las federaciones deportivas; las asociaciones de consumidores y usuarios; así como cualesquiera otras reguladas por leyes especiales.
Las asociaciones constituidas para fines exclusivamente religiosos por las iglesias, confesiones y comunidades religiosas se regirán por lo dispuesto en los tratados internacionales y en las leyes específicas, sin perjuicio de la aplicación supletoria de las disposiciones de la presente Ley Orgánica.

Once they are registered, religious groups have legal status as religious entities. The registration procedure starts with a written request submitted to the RRE by the representatives of the religious community. In accordance with the Religious Freedom Act, this application must be accompanied by an authenticated document containing information on the foundation or establishment of the organisation in Spain, its name and other identification data, a declaration of its religious purpose, bylaws which include details of the organisation's representative bodies and conditions for a valid designation thereof.

Ley Orgánica 7/1980, de 5 de julio de Libertad Religiosa

Artículo quinto.
1. Las Iglesias, Confesiones y Comunidades religiosas y sus Federaciones gozarán de personalidad jurídica una vez inscritas en el correspondiente Registro público, que se crea, a tal efecto, en el Ministerio de Justicia
2. La inscripción se practicará en virtud de solicitud, acompañada de documento fehaciente en el que consten su fundación o establecimiento en España, expresión de sus fines religiosos, denominación y demás datos de identificación, régimen de funcionamiento y órganos representativos, con expresión de sus facultades y de los requisitos para su válida designación.
3. La cancelación de los asientos relativos a una determinada Entidad religiosa sólo podrá llevarse a cabo a petición de sus órganos representativos o en cumplimiento de sentencia judicial firme.

The Royal Decree 594/2015 of 3 July regulating the Registry of Religious Entities (RER), which entered into force on 1 November 2015, has implemented these requirements.[16]

The most controversial of these requirements is the declaration of religious purposes ("expresión de sus fines religiosos"). According to the Constitutional Court,[17] the State should not assess religious purposes. Thus, registration can be refused only if denominations do not fulfil the requirements or if it is legally proven (for example by a legal judgment) that these groups use illegal methods or seek illegal goals.

Real Decreto 594/2015, de 3 de julio, por el que se regula el Registro de Entidades Religiosas.

Artículo 4. Derecho de inscripción.
2. Solo podrá denegarse la inscripción cuando no se reúnan los requisitos establecidos en la Ley Orgánica 7/1980, de 5 de julio, de Libertad Religiosa o en el presente real decreto.

Registering in the RRE brings with it only few legal effects for religious groups, namely, a) it is evidence of their legal personality as religious groups (art. 5.1 Religious Freedom Act); b) they then have the opportunity to organise themselves with complete autonomy. For example, religious groups do not have to be democratically organised, a compulsory requirement for associations.

Ley Orgánica 1/2002, de 22 de marzo reguladora del Derecho de Asociación

Artículo 2.5: La organización interna y el funcionamiento de las asociaciones deben ser democráticos, con pleno respeto al pluralismo. (…)

Ley Orgánica 7/1980, de 5 de julio de Libertad Religiosa

Artículo 6:
Uno. Las Iglesias, Confesiones y Comunidades religiosas inscritas tendrán plena autonomía y podrán establecer sus propias normas de organización, régimen interno y régimen de su personal. (…)

16 Royal Decree 594/2015, of 3 July. See https://www.boe.es/boe/dias/2015/08/01/pdfs/BOE-A-2015-8643.pdf.

17 Judgment 46/2001 of 15 February (BOE no. 65, of 16 March 2001).

c) regarding their labour relations, registered religious groups can include clauses safeguarding their religious identity.

Artículo 6:
Uno: (…) En dichas normas, así como en las que regulen las instituciones creadas por aquéllas para la realización de sus fines, podrán incluir cláusulas de salvaguarda de su identidad religiosa y carácter propio, así como del debido respeto a sus creencias, sin perjuicio del respeto de los derechos y libertades reconocidos por la Constitución, y en especial de los de libertad, igualdad y no discriminación.

d) According to Organic Law 4/2000, on the rights and freedoms of foreigners, their foreign religious ministers do not need work permits as long as their activities are of a religious nature. This is the case with many foreign imams that come for Ramadan to any registered mosque.

Ley Orgánica 4/2000, de 11 de enero, sobre derechos y libertades de los extranjeros en España y su integración social.
BOE núm. 10, de 12 de enero de 2000

Artículo 41. Excepciones al permiso de trabajo.
"1. No será necesaria la obtención de permiso de trabajo para el ejercicio de las actividades siguientes: […] h) Los ministros, religiosos o representantes de las diferentes iglesias y confesiones, debidamente inscritas en el Registro de Entidades Religiosas, en tanto limiten su actividad a funciones estrictamente religiosas …".

In accordance with article 26 of Royal Decree 594/2015, the Registry of Religious Entities is divided into these Sections: a) The General Section, which includes Religious Communities which have not signed a Cooperation Agreement with the State. b) The Special Section, which includes Religious Communities that have signed a Cooperation Agreement with the State c) The Historical Section, which includes religious groups (or their bodies) whose registrations have been cancelled.

1.2.3 *"Deeply Rooted" Denominations*

In accordance with article 7 of the Religious Freedom Act of 1980 the State may establish Cooperation Agreements with those registered religious entities which, due to their scope or number of followers, have obtained the status of "deeply rooted" (*notorio arraigo*) denominations. As we have said, this legal imprecision for many years permitted this decision to be adopted by a consultative body appointed by the Ministry of Justice (now under the Ministry of Presidency), the Advisory Board for Religious Freedom (CALR). But, finally, in 2015 the Government issued a Royal Decree to clarify and objectify this requirement (Royal Decree 593/2015). This purpose is declared in the preamble:

Real Decreto 593/2015, de 3 de julio, por el que se regula la declaración de notorio arraigo de las confesiones religiosas en España
BOE» núm. 183, de 1 de agosto de 2015,
La declaración de notorio arraigo debe abarcar unas notas comunes que caractericen a cualquier iglesia, [...] que deben conocerse con carácter previo por parte de los diversos grupos religiosos, pero también por parte de la sociedad. Debe permitir acreditar que goza de una presencia estable y acreditada en el tiempo en España mediante su inscripción en el Registro de Entidades Religiosas, o bien en algún país extranjero, pero que en todo caso aporte la nota de estabilidad y permanencia en el tiempo. Asimismo, el arraigo debe asociarse a la presencia activa en la sociedad española y su implantación en el territorio de varias comunidades autónomas y con un número representativo de entidades y lugares de culto inscritos en el Registro de Entidades Religiosas. Igualmente, debe contar con una estructura interna y representación adecuada a su propia organización.

These requirements were specified in art. 3 of the Royal Decree:

Artículo 3. Requisitos.
Para la declaración de notorio arraigo en España a que se refiere el artículo 7.1 de la Ley Orgánica 7/1980, de 5 de julio, las iglesias, confesiones o comunidades religiosas deberán reunir los requisitos siguientes:
a) Llevar inscritas en el Registro de Entidades Religiosas treinta años, salvo que la entidad acredite un reconocimiento en el extranjero de, al menos, sesenta años de antigüedad y lleve inscrita en el citado Registro durante un periodo de quince años.
b) Acreditar su presencia en, al menos, diez comunidades autónomas y/o ciudades de Ceuta y Melilla.
c) Tener 100 inscripciones o anotaciones en el Registro de Entidades Religiosas, entre entes inscribibles y lugares de culto, o un número inferior cuando se trate de entidades o lugares de culto de especial relevancia por su actividad y número de miembros.

d) Contar con una estructura y representación adecuada y suficiente para su organización a los efectos de la declaración de notorio arraigo.
e) Acreditar su presencia y participación activa en la sociedad española.

Once they have obtained this designation, deeply rooted denominations get three further legal advantages: a) the possibility of reaching a Cooperation Agreement with the State; b) the right to have a representative member on the Advisory Commission of Religious Freedom[18] (c) their forms of marriage celebration will have civil effects.[19]

The religious confessions recognised for their well-known roots in Spain are Jews and Protestants (in 1984), Muslims (in 1989), the Church of Jesus Christ of Latter-day Saints or Mormons (in 2003), Jehovah's Witnesses (in 2006), Buddhists (in 2007) and the Orthodox Church (in 2010). But so far, these last four groups have not signed a Cooperation Agreement with the State.

1.2.4 *Denominations That Have Signed a Cooperation Agreement with the State*

Only deeply rooted entities have the ability to sign Cooperation Agreements with the State. At this point, we may distinguish between the Cooperation Agreements signed by the State with Catholic Church (which are international treaties) and those signed by the State with Protestantism, Judaism and Islam (which are ordinary laws).

Once their well-established roots were registered and recognised in 1989, the Islamic communities began negotiations with the State to define the content of this Agreement. Unlike the other two recognised confessions, the Muslim communities were doubly represented, since two federations were established: the Spanish Federation of Islamic Religious Entities (FEERI) and the Union of Islamic Communities of Spain (UCIDE).[20] Although initially both FEERI and UCIDE presented their own projects to the Government, the Ministry of Justice required them to be a single negotiating partner, and ordered the entities to form a single body to conclude the last part of the Agreement negotiation. Thus, FEERI and UCIDE agreed on 18 February 1992 to create the Islamic Commission of Spain (CIE).

18 Royal Decree 932/2013, of November 29, on the Advisory Commission of Religious Freedom (BOE núm. 300, of 16 December 2013). Art. 8.

19 Law 15/2015 of 2 July of Optional Jurisdiction.

20 When the negotiating process was begun in 1991, of the 40 registered Muslim communities, 15 belonged to FEERI, 17 to UCIDE and eight were not attached to either of the two. See Fernández-Coronado (1995: 82).

1.3 Administrative Bodies Related to Denominations

In Spain, relations between public authorities and religions come under the deputy director of Relations with Denominations which used to be under the Ministry of Justice but nowadays (since February 2020) it is under the Ministry of Presidency. Also, the Register of Religious Entities (RRE) comes under this ministry.

However, there are other ministries that deal with religious affairs. For example, the Ministry of the Interior deals with spiritual guidance in prisons, the Ministry of Finance with funding or tax benefits for some religious groups, and the Labour Ministry handles the social security funds of priests, imams, rabbis and other faith ministers.

Other administrative bodies that engage with religious communities are:

- The Advisory Commission for Religious Freedom (*Comisión Asesora de la Libertad Religiosa*, CALR), a consultative body appointed by the Ministry of Justice. The Commission's purpose is to undertake studies, reports and proposals for all those issues applicable to the Religious Freedom Act, with emphasis on the preparation and reporting of Cooperation Agreements.[21]
- The "Pluralism and Coexistence" Foundation (*Fundación Pluralismo y Convivencia*), a public Foundation created in December 2005 by decision of the Council of Ministers on the proposal of the Ministry of Justice (since February 2020, under the Ministry of the Presidency). Its main objective is to support cultural, educational and social integration projects presented by religious communities which have signed a Cooperation Agreement with the State (this excludes the Catholic Church which has its own specific funding from the State). The mission of this foundation is "to encourage the recognition and the accommodation of religious diversity as basic elements to fully guaranteeing freedom of religion and enabling an appropriate environment for living together. Its main objectives are: a) to contribute to the implementation of programmes and projects by non-Catholic religious denominations with an agreement of cooperation with the Spanish State or with well-established roots in Spain related to the promotion of the full exercise of the right to religious freedom; b) To improve knowledge about religious diversity in Spain, its impact and associated needs; c) To improve public management of religious diversity, and d) To help building an informed public opinion that is tolerant of religious plurality".[22]

---

21 Royal Decree 932/2013, of 29 November, which regulates the Advisory Commission on Religious Freedom.

22 See http://www.pluralismoyconvivencia.es/ (accessed 3 March 2021).

Real Decreto 45/2021, de 26 de enero de 2021. Estatutos de la Fundación Pluralismo y Convivencia. Boletín Oficial del Estado (28 de enero 2021).
Fines de la Fundación
Artículo 7. Fines. 1. Son fines de la Fundación contribuir a la ejecución de programas y proyectos de carácter cultural, educativo, social, y de promoción de las condiciones necesarias para el ejercicio efectivo del derecho de libertad religiosa, por parte de las confesiones no católicas con acuerdo de cooperación con el Estado español o con notorio arraigo en España, así como la ejecución y promoción de actividades relacionadas con la investigación, la sensibilización y el asesoramiento en la gestión de la diversidad religiosa.

- The Office of Relations with the Holy See under the Sub-Secretary of Foreign Affairs and Cooperation (Ministry of Foreign Affairs and Cooperation), which is dedicated to some matters related to the Holy See.[23]
- The Regional Government of Catalonia has the General Directorate for Religious Affairs, whose functions are: a) assisting religious bodies in Catalonia; b) applying government orders to the representative bodies of the various religious faiths in Catalonia and ensuring they are complied with; c) acting as a representative of the Catalan Regional Government to the religious bodies; d) conducting studies, writing reports and promoting awareness-raising activities regarding religious affairs; e) establishing and maintaining relations with the heads of institutions for matters concerning religion; f) participating in the management of the Registry of Religious Bodies in coordination with the General State Administration; g) any similar function entrusted to it; h) the recognition and institutional representation of faiths. Also, the General Directorate has published a map indicating the places of worship and organisational structure of the main faiths within the territory.[24]
- In addition, the Regional Government of Catalonia has an Advisory Council for Religious Diversity, composed of 14 experts, whose functions are: a) advising and informing the head of the department of the Catalan Regional Government competent in religious affairs about the issues brought before it; b) proposing action or plans that it deems appropriate within the context of relations with the various churches, faiths and reli-

---

23 But also with the embassy of the Order of Malta and some other items like Pious Charitable Deed of Holy Places (*Obra pía de los Santos Lugares*). See Ferreiro (2008).

24 http://justicia.gencat.cat/ca/ambits/afers-religiosos/estudis/Mapa/ (accessed 3 March 2020).

gious communities that are active in Catalonia; c) advising on and, at the request of the head of the department of the Catalan Regional Government competent in religious affairs, giving support to the collaborative or cooperative partnerships requiring the involvement of the Government or Parliament of Catalonia in State institutions or international organisations.[25]

25 See http://justicia.gencat.cat/ca/ambits/afers-religiosos/consell-assessor/ (accessed 3 March 2020).

CHAPTER 2

Relations between the State and Islam

2.1 Historical Relations

For Spanish society, the memory of the splendour of Al-Andalus' culture and civilisation acts to a certain degree as a burden in the present. Its legacy appears as a constant for Spanish society that refers it back to what is Arab and Muslim but at the same time is an *interference* between the perception of the past and the living of the present, a past which, on being reclaimed by literature and other genres, frequently ends up being reified. The fact is that a good number of the images with which Spanish society constructs its image of Islam are derived from its conflicted historical relationship with its neighbour, Morocco, during which there has been a gradual accumulation of stereotypes which have strengthened the antagonisms between the two societies.

Today, as a product of the immigration of people of Maghreb and African origin to Spain, which began in the 1960s and 1970s, a new Islamic presence has been formed: a presence that breaks the perception of an otherness understood thus far as a spatial and historically distant reality. Statistical evidence confirms that the majority of Muslims in Spain are foreigners. Nevertheless, there are numerous indicators that show the settling-in of such groups (immigrant communities with a long presence, naturalisations and new generations), the development of associations (which essentially bring together converts to Islam) and their historical rooting (the populations of Ceuta and Melilla of Moroccan origin). Despite this, the social perception of this presence remains directly linked to North African, sub-Saharan and Asiatic migrations marking it on account of its foreign character as "the religion of foreigners" rather than as a "religious minority".

The construction of a Muslim space in Spain is closely related to the development of relations between the State and religious confessions. During the Franco period (1939–1975), the regime's Catholic confessional character prevented the recognition of other religions. It was not until 1967 that the first post-Civil War law on religious freedom recognised the possibility of a controlled practice of religions other than Catholicism. In 1968 the first Muslim association was created in Melilla, a logical product of the cultural substrate of this North African city, and in 1971 the Muslim Association of Spain was formed. The political transition opened a new space of freedoms for Spanish society, among them that of religion, which favoured the development of Muslim associations particularly among groups of Spanish converts in Andalusia. In the 1980s the first prayer halls set up by immigrant groups, basically Moroccans but also sub-Saharans and Pakistanis, began to appear as the result of the process of settlement of migratory flows.

Counting numbers in religious affiliations is prohibited by the 1978 Spanish Constitution;[1] therefore, the number of Muslims in Spain is the subject of estimates that are not always based on reliable data. According to official statistics,[2] the figure for legal foreigner residents in 2019 is 1,103,925. The largest Muslim group in Spain is still Moroccans (795,619, compared to 782,295 in 2018), followed by Pakistanis (85,238; 80,901 in 2018) and Senegalese (64,845; 63,136 in 2018). To this figure we should add the total number of those naturalised between 1968 and 2019 (396,293), so reaching a total of 1,500,218 Muslims in Spain (1,437,717 in 2018).

Faced with these data extracted from official statistics, the data provided by the Andalusian Observatory [*Observatorio Andalusi*] (a body set up in 2003 by the Union of Islamic Communities in Spain [*Unión de Comunidades Islámicas de España*]) must also be included.[3] Their estimates often offer higher figures. On this occasion, this observatory considers that 42 per cent of Muslims in Spain are Spanish citizens, part of a total figure of 2,091,656 Muslims in the country (4 per cent of the Spanish population). In this figure, the Observatory includes naturalisations (352,436), the residents of Ceuta and Melilla (72,917), those born to Muslim families in Spain (555,266)[4] and converts (called *naturales*, which make up a total of 26,072 individuals).[5]

Beyond the difference between the two estimates, the truth is that practically half of the Muslim population in Spain has acquired Spanish nationality, or

1 Actually, what the Spanish Constitution prohibits is not asking but forcing someone to answer about their religion. CE article. 16.2: 2: "No one can be compelled to make statements about their religion, beliefs or ideologies". See chapter 1.1.2.

2 See www.ine.es, accessed 26 January 2020.

3 Observatorio Andalusi, *Estudio demográfico de la población musulmana: Explotación estadística del censo de ciudadanos musulmanes en España referido a fecha 31 de diciembre de 2018* (*Demographic Study of the Census of Muslim Citizens in Spain Conducted 31 December 2019*) (Madrid: Unión de Comunidades Islámicas de España, 2019), http://observatorio.hispanomuslim.es, accessed 19 February 2020.

4 These data should be questioned since Spanish citizenship is not obtained automatically by being born in Spain if both parents are foreigners.

5 The Andalusian Observatory does not provide any information regarding the origin of this calculation for the number of people who have converted to Islam. If we compare these estimates with the Observatory's previous reports, the number of converts consistently represents 3% of the total of Spanish Muslim citizens (or "*hispanomusulmanes*").

that it is ready to obtain it shortly, either by birth or residence.[6] Until 2009 the number of naturalisations granted in Spain to foreigners of Muslim countries grew steadily, except in 2017 when the number of grants of Spanish nationality was reduced for administrative reasons. In 2019, a total of 45,897 people from Muslim countries obtained Spanish nationality.

A specific study of the main reasons for granting nationality to the two main Muslim groups (Moroccans and Pakistanis) between the years 2018 and 2019 is indicative of the degree of settlement of this population in Spanish society. The two main reasons for obtaining Spanish citizenship are having been born in Spain if one of the parents is Spanish (*ius soli*) or to document a ten-year long stay in Spanish territory (*arraigo*). The other third reason, that of marriage to a Spaniard, constitutes a very small percentage among these two groups, which indicates the high degree of endogamy.

Código Civil
Real Decreto de 24 de julio de 1889 por el que se publica el Código Civil

Artículo 17. 1. Son españoles de origen:
a) Los nacidos de padre o madre españoles.
b) Los nacidos en España de padres extranjeros si, al menos, uno de ellos hubiera nacido también en España. Se exceptúan los hijos de funcionario diplomático o consular acreditado en España.
c) Los nacidos en España de padres extranjeros, si ambos carecieren de nacionalidad o si la legislación de ninguno de ellos atribuye al hijo una nacionalidad.
d) Los nacidos en España cuya filiación no resulte determinada. A estos efectos, se presumen nacidos en territorio español los menores de edad cuyo primer lugar conocido de estancia sea territorio español. [...]
Artículo 22.
1. Para la concesión de la nacionalidad por residencia se requiere que ésta haya durado diez años. Serán suficientes cinco años para los que hayan obtenido la condición de refugiado y dos años cuando se trate de nacionales de origen de países iberoamericanos, Andorra, Filipinas, Guinea Ecuatorial o Portugal o de sefardíes.
2. Bastará el tiempo de residencia de un año para:
a) El que haya nacido en territorio español.
b) El que no haya ejercitado oportunamente la facultad de optar.

6 90.2% of Moroccans and 75.2% of Pakistanis living in Spain have permanent residence permits (2019).

c) El que haya estado sujeto legalmente a la tutela, guarda o acogimiento de un ciudadano o institución españoles durante dos años consecutivos, incluso si continuare en esta situación en el momento de la solicitud.
d) El que al tiempo de la solicitud llevare un año casado con español o española y no estuviere separado legalmente o de hecho.
e) El viudo o viuda de española o español, si a la muerte del cónyuge no existiera separación legal o de hecho.
f) El nacido fuera de España de padre o madre, abuelo o abuela, que originariamente hubieran sido españoles.
3. En todos los casos, la residencia habrá de ser legal, continuada e inmediatamente anterior a la petición.
A los efectos de lo previsto en el párrafo d) del apartado anterior, se entenderá que tiene residencia legal en España el cónyuge que conviva con funcionario diplomático o consular español acreditado en el extranjero.
4. El interesado deberá justificar, en el expediente regulado por la legislación del Registro Civil, buena conducta cívica y suficiente grado de integración en la sociedad española.
5. La concesión o denegación de la nacionalidad por residencia deja a salvo la vía judicial contencioso-administrativa.

2.2 The Cooperation Agreement with the Islamic Commission of Spain

Once the federations that represented Muslims, Protestants and Jews had received their "deeply rooted" status, those three denominations negotiated three different but quite similar Cooperation Agreements with the State that, once they were reached, were passed as laws in the Parliament (Laws 24, 25 and 26 of 10 November 1992 including the Cooperation Agreement between the Spanish State and the Islamic Commission of Spain).

As these denominations are not part of a State (such as the Catholic Church being related to the Vatican) the Cooperation Agreements they have signed with the State do not have the legal form of international treaties, but they are ordinary laws, which can be repealed, suspended or amended by subsequent ordinary laws. The special rights enshrined in these Cooperation Agreements affect only the religious communities that belong to the representative bodies that have signed those Agreements with the State.

Ley 26/1992, de 10 de noviembre, por la que se aprueba el Acuerdo de Cooperación del Estado con la Comisión Islámica de España

Exposición de Motivos:
"… La Ley Orgánica de Libertad Religiosa establece la posibilidad de que el Estado concrete su cooperación con las Confesiones o Comunidades religiosas, mediante la adopción de Acuerdos o Convenios de Cooperación, cuando aquéllas, debidamente inscritas en el Registro de Entidades Religiosas, hayan alcanzado en la sociedad española, además, un arraigo que, por el número de sus creyentes y por la extensión de su credo, resulte evidente o notorio. En este caso se encuentra la religión islámica, de tradición secular en nuestro país, con relevante importancia en la formación de la identidad española, representada por distintas Comunidades de dicha confesión, inscritas en el Registro de Entidades Religiosas e integradas en alguna de las dos Federaciones igualmente inscritas, denominadas Federación Española de Entidades Religiosas Islámicas y Unión de Comunidades Islámicas de España, que, a su vez, han constituido una entidad religiosa inscrita con la denominación de «Comisión Islámica de España», como órgano representativo del islam en España ante el Estado para la negociación, firma y seguimiento de los acuerdos adoptados".

The signing in 1992 of the Cooperation Agreement between the Spanish State and the Islamic Commission of Spain marked a milestone in the recognition of the Muslim presence in Spain. This Agreement was to establish a framework that was to serve as a guide in organising Muslim religious practice with reference to all relevant factors which was adapted to legal principles in force in Spain. Among its most noteworthy aspects is the fact that the Agreement defined the Islamic community's structure, making the Islamic Commission of Spain (CIE) (made up of representatives of the great Muslim federations, the *Federación Española de Entidades Religiosas Islámicas* (Spanish Federation of Islamic Religious Entities, FEERI), created in 1989; and the *Unión de Comunidades Islámicas de España* (Union of Islamic Communities of Spain, UCIDE), created in 1990)) the representative and organising body of Islam in Spain, which was to manage different aspects of religious practice as well as to train and appoint religious staff, certify the development and execution of certain religious observances, and supervise the incorporation of Islamic religious education into the national educational system.

In terms of the content of the Cooperation Agreement, it responded to the interests of the parties signing it. For the State, it served to clarify a situation that had been very complex involving the arrival of Muslim immigrants, and to determine who represents the Islamic community in its relations with the government. For Spanish Muslims, the most significant factor was recognition by the State of the community's presence and its social rooting in Spain, and the granting of rights like those enjoyed by the Catholic Church as a way of righting what had always been seen as a historic injustice.

Nonetheless almost thirty years after the Agreement's signing, the balance of its application is limited.[7] This is usually explained as being for two reasons: disputes between the two constituent federations that make up the Islamic Commission of Spain, and that derive from the unification imposed by the Spanish State for the signing of the Agreement; and the limited political interest in developing the content of the Agreement and confronting public controversies that may appear. The truth is that since this Agreement was signed the reality of the Muslim community has changed a great deal, new needs have appeared, and new priorities have been established. Without being able to affirm that this legal framework has become obsolete, it can be said that it is inadequate to solve questions such as about the Islamic dress codes or the training of imams and others Muslim leaders.

2.3 The Islamic Commission of Spain

One of the most significant elements of the 1992 Cooperation Agreement was the identification of an institution that was to be the representative of the Muslim community before public administrations. The dual character of the Islamic Commission of Spain (the sum of FEERI and UCIDE) influenced how it functioned internally in the following decades.

ESTATUTOS DE LA "COMISIÓN ISLÁMICA DE ESPAÑA" (18 de febrero de 1992)[8]
Artículo 1º.—La FEERI y la UCIDE constituyen una Entidad islámica denominada "COMISIÓN ISLÁMICA DE ESPAÑA", para la negociación, firma y seguimiento del Acuerdo de cooperación con el Estado. A tal efecto se inscribirá en el Registro de Entidades Religiosas a fin de tener personalidad jurídica propia. A dicha entidad podrán incorporarse las Comunidades islámicas, inscritas en el mencionado Registro que lo deseen, sin otro requisito que la aceptación de los contenidos del Acuerdo de cooperación, directamente o por conducto de alguna de las mencionadas Federaciones, y sean admitidas por la Comisión permanente que podrá denegar la admisión por motivos de índole religiosa.

7 See Ferreiro (2017).
8 Nowadays not in force, as they were modified in 2016. See Mantecón (2016).

Artículo 2º.—Denominación: La Entidad Islámica se denomina "COMISIÓN ISLÁMICA DE ESPAÑA".
Artículo 3º.—Domicilio: La "Comisión Islámica de España", fija su domicilio en Madrid, calle Anastasio Herrero, número 7 y calle Salvador de Madariaga, s/nº.
Artículo 4º.—FINES. El fin de la "Comisión Islámica de España", es la representación de las entidades religiosas islámicas a que se refiere el artículo 1º, a los efectos expresados en él, para impulsar y facilitar la práctica del Islam en España, de acuerdo con los preceptos del Corán y de la Sunna.

The statutes of the CIE included the creation of two hierarchical entities: the Permanent Commission and the General Secretariat. The first would be made up of six members (three from each federation), and the second of the general secretaries of FEERI and UCIDE.

ESTATUTOS DE LA "COMISIÓN ISLÁMICA DE ESPAÑA" (18 de febrero de 1992)
Artículo 5º.—ÓRGANOS RECTORES-Serán la Comisión Permanente y la Secretaría General.
Artículo 6º.—La Comisión permanente, como órgano colegiado, estará integrada inicialmente por seis miembros, tres por cada Federación, que serán designados por las federaciones respectivas, de conformidad con sus correspondientes normas estatutarias, por un periodo de tres años. Las Comunidades islámicas que se incorporen directamente a la "Comisión Islámica de España", podrán tener su propia representación en la Comisión permanente. A tal efecto, cada diez Comunidades podrán nombrar, de acuerdo con sus normas estatutarias, una representación común que constará de tres miembros.

FACULTADES: La Comisión Permanente tendrá las siguientes facultades:
– El nombramiento de los dos Secretarios Generales, uno por cada Federación representada, a propuesta de cada Federación.
– La modificación de los presentes Estatutos.
– Aprobación del presupuesto y cuentas anuales del ejercicio.
– Deliberación de los asuntos que sobre la aplicación ejecución y seguimiento del Acuerdo de Cooperación con el Estado Español, le sean sometidos a su consideración.
– La admisión de nuevas comunidades que lo soliciten.

– Cualquier facultad que le sea inherente a la finalidad de la Comisión Islámica de España.
La Comisión permanente se reunirá, al menos, una vez al año. Sus acuerdos y decisiones se adoptarán por mayoría absoluta de sus miembros, previo el acuerdo también mayoritario de los representantes de cada Federación y, en su caso el de los representantes de las agrupaciones de diez Comunidades a que se refiere el párrafo 2º de este artículo.
Artículo 7º.—Secretaría General. Estará integrada inicialmente por dos Secretarios, un Secretario, designado por cada una de las 2 Federaciones constituyentes de la "Comisión Islámica de España", y, en su caso, por otro Secretario, por cada agrupación de diez Comunidades de las expresadas en el párrafo 2º del artículo anterior.

FUNCIONES.
Las funciones de los Secretarios serán:
– Ostentar la representación legal de la "Comisión Islámica de España".
– Ejecutar los acuerdos adoptados por la Comisión Permanente.
– Convocar a la Comisión Permanente fijando el orden del día de sus reuniones.
– Elaborar el presupuesto.
– Certificar de forma mancomunada los necesarios certificados y acreditaciones.

Created in September 1989, the FEERI was originally formed by associations of Spanish converts to Islam. The former founder and president of the first Muslim federation was Mansur Escudero (1947–2010), who also promoted the creation of the *Junta Islámica*, one of the most active Islamic entities that developed the main website portal on Islam in Spain (*Webislam*) in the 1990s. Originally, FEERI was a heterodox group formed by various Islamic tendencies (orthodox Sunnis, Sufi inspired groups and even Shi'a), with a directorate based in Cordova (Andalusia) and strongly linked with Muslim communities in Ceuta and Melilla. After Escudero's death, Mounir Benjelloun became the new president. The Spanish intelligence services place Benjelloun within the orbit of the Moroccan movement *Al Adl wal Ihsane* (Justice and Spirituality).

The UCIDE was created at the initiative of Riay Tatary Bakri (1948–2020), who in 1970 arrived in Spain from Syria, and who a year later would create the *Asociación Musulmana de España* (Muslim Association of Spain). The Union of Islamic Communities of Spain was created in April 1990, presenting itself as an alternative to the FEERI, after the recognition of the well-known roots of Islam in Spain. Even though Tatary always maintained close relations with the representatives of the Muslim Brotherhood in Europe, the UCIDE constitutes a heterodox network of entities spread throughout the Spanish territory and is not institutionally linked to this Islamist-inspired movement. The relations between the president of the UCIDE and the Spanish political institutions have been friendlier and more open to dialogue than those maintained by the FEERI, which used to be more critical and demanding.

The struggle for the representation of Islam in Spain has been constant throughout recent decades, and the two federations have tried to have new Islamic entities registered. In August 2000, there were 153 Muslim religious associations in Spain registered in the Registry of Religious Entities. Fifty-three of them belonged to the Spanish Federation of Islamic Religious Entities (FEERI) and 65 to the Union of Islamic Communities of Spain (UCIDE), while another 35 were not federated. This balance would progressively move in favour of the UCIDE, which has benefited from the notable increase in the registration of Muslim entities. The exponential registration of new entities showed the changes in balance between the two federations, but at the same time led to the emergence of a whole new associative context that was organised alongside the previous two federations.

At the beginning of January 2021, the Islamic associative landscape in Spain was organised around 1,789 entities listed in the Ministry of Presidency's Register of Religious Entities.[9] Only 1,215 of them belong to the Islamic Commission of Spain (CIE)—thus only they enjoy of the benefits of the Cooperation Agreement. Of them, 775 are attached to UCIDE, 217 are linked to FEERI and 440 belong to new Muslim federations that belong to the Islamic Commission of Spain. There is a total of 49 Islamic federations in Spain that belong to CIE, which groups local communities regionally. There are 357 entities not attached to any federation that belongs to CIE

After the incorporation in 2011 of new federations in the Islamic Commission of Spain (approved by Royal Decree 1384/2011 on 14 October), it did not make sense to maintain this duality between UCIDE and FEERI. The reformulation of the Islamic Commission of Spain (CIE) on 18 September 2015 meant de facto ending this dual structure, which came into force four years later, and allowed the election of a president and an executive commission composed of members of the different federations present in Spanish Islam. On 20 October 2016, the Registry of Religious Entities recorded an amendment to the statutes of the Islamic Commission of Spain and its new legal represent-

9 Source: Registry of Religious Entities. Ministry of Presidency (https://maper.mjusticia.gob.es/), accessed 19 January 2021.

ation.[10] The reform created a Standing Committee as the representative body, with 25 members (composed of representatives of the different Islamic federations, and in which the UCIDE would have the majority of members), and a Board of Directors including a President and 14 members. It also established the legal opportunity to set up Regional Delegations and Technical Committees.[11] This process was complex, because the Spanish State raised doubts whether veteran leader Riay Tatary, who chairs the UCIDE, was the president of the Islamic Commission of Spain until his death in April 2020. On 18 July 2020, the CIE's new board of directors was created under the presidency of Ayman Adlbi. For the first time, two women sit on the new board of directors, and a women's commission will be created.

ESTATUTOS DE LA COMISIÓN ISLÁMICA DE ESPAÑA (septiembre 2016)
Artículo 4. Fines.
1. La finalidad de la CIE es ostentar la representación única, conforme a lo dispuesto en el Acuerdo de Cooperación del Estado con la CIE, contenido en la ley 26/1992, de 10 de noviembre, ante el Estado Español, de las entidades religiosas islámicas citadas en el Artículo 1º, para la adecuada interlocución con las Administraciones de Estado en todo lo referente al desarrollo y al ejercicio de la libertad religiosa, y en particular, para la negociación, seguimiento, desarrollo y aplicación del Acuerdo de Cooperación firmado con el Estado Español y de otros acuerdos sectoriales, autonómicos y/o normas que sean de aplicación a los musulmanes de España.
2. Impulsar y facilitar la práctica del Islam en España de acuerdo con los preceptos del Corán y de la Sunna.
3. El diálogo con otras instituciones para favorecer la convivencia en armonía y plenitud de todas las personas con diferentes creencias y convicciones.
4. El cumplimiento de sus fines se hará dentro del marco constitucional y legal de España en el ejercicio del derecho a la libertad religiosa y del respeto a los principios de convivencia constitucional.
5. La CIE se define como una entidad sin ánimo de lucro.

10 The text of the CIE statutes can be consulted here: https://www.comisionislamica.org/wp-content/uploads/2020/10/Estatutos-CIE-2016.pdf, accessed on 18 May 2020.

11 The CIE organisation chart can be consulted here: https://comisionislamica.org/organizacion/, accessed on 23 October 2020.

The Cooperation Agreement with the Islamic Commission did not contemplate its financing from the State budget. However, it was evident that it was necessary to establish a mechanism to support the development of the institution that would assume the leadership and representation of Islam in Spain. Through the *Pluralism and Coexistence Foundation*, the CIE receives annual funding that is intended for its operation. The amount dedicated in 2019 to the Islamic Commission is the same as in the previous year: 330,000 €. In addition to that amount, another 108,566 € was awarded to projects submitted by the local Muslim communities. It is important to remember that in 2017 the Spanish State decided to audit all Muslim, Jewish, Protestant and Catholic groups that receive public subsidies.

CHAPTER 3

Muslims and Citizenship

As in any system governed by the rule of law, Muslims have the same rights as any other citizen (Spanish Constitution article 14).[1] Among the manifestations of religious freedom referred to in Organic Law 7/1980 is the right to gather for religious purposes.[2] Protection of personal privacy should also be mentioned, which implies the prohibition on forcing anyone to testify about their religious convictions (Spanish Constitution, article 16),[3] which affects the preparation of official registers or censuses.

It is not only individuals who benefit from religious freedom but also religious confessions, as is the case with Islam. An Islamic entity, like any other religious group, has several options for obtaining legal personality.[4] Even though at present most Muslim communities have chosen enrolment in the Register of Religious Entities (RRE) in the Ministry of the Presidency, there are still some Islamic communities that have decided to remain in an undefined legal situation. As we have just said, among the entities that have decided to register in the RRE, only those that are attached to the Islamic Commission of Spain (CIE) will be able to benefit from the Cooperation Agreement signed in 1992.

The fact that a significant number of the Muslim population in Spain are still foreigners, and with a nationality that is not a European Union one, conditions their access to some political rights (such as the right to vote and to be elected in local elections). According to article 23 of our Constitution, only Spaniards are entitled to these rights, except in cases which may be established by treaty or by law concerning the right to vote and the right to be elected in municipal elections, in accordance with the principle of reciprocity.

Constitución Española (1978)

Artículo 23:
1. “Los ciudadanos tienen el derecho a participar en los asuntos públicos, directamente o por medio de representantes, libremente elegidos en elecciones periódicas por sufragio universal.

1 See chapter 1.1.1.
2 Ibid.
3 See chapter 1.1.2.
4 See chapter 1.2. Four Types of Legal Recognition.

2. Asimismo, tienen derecho a acceder en condiciones de igualdad a las funciones y cargos públicos, con los requisitos que señalen las leyes".

Artículo 13.
1. Los extranjeros gozarán en España de las libertades públicas que garantiza el presente Título en los términos que establezcan los tratados y la ley.
2. Solamente los españoles serán titulares de los derechos reconocidos en el artículo 23, salvo lo que, atendiendo a criterios de reciprocidad, pueda establecerse por tratado o ley para el derecho de sufragio activo y pasivo en las elecciones municipales.

This structural factor determines in a very obvious way which kind of "Muslim vote" can be thought of in Spain. In the case of Ceuta and Melilla, the two Spanish cities in North Africa that have a significant Muslim population, the political parties are very aware of this factor. But in the rest of Spain, this issue has hardly been considered. This is confirmed by the experience of the first Spanish political party that expressed a Muslim ideology, PRUNE (Renaissance Party and Union of Spain), which was created in Granada in 2009, and which met with little success in some municipal elections.

CHAPTER 4

Mosques and Prayer Houses

4.1 Patterns of Social Visibility

In accordance with the Cooperation Agreement between the Spanish State and the Islamic commission of Spain, mosques must fulfil two requirements: being used exclusively and regularly for prayer, religious education or training and spiritual guidance; and being certified as such mosques by the competent Islamic community, with the agreement of the Islamic Commission of Spain.

Ley 26/1992, de 10 de noviembre, por la que se aprueba el Acuerdo de Cooperación del Estado con la Comisión Islámica de España

Artículo 2.1:
A todos los efectos legales, son Mezquitas o lugares de culto de las Comunidades Islámicas pertenecientes a la Comisión Islámica de España los edificios o locales destinados de forma exclusiva a la práctica habitual de la oración, formación o asistencia religiosa islámica, cuando así se certifique por la Comunidad respectiva, con la conformidad de dicha Comisión.

These mosques have some legal privileges such as their inviolability; or in case of expropriation that the religious authorities (Islamic Commission of Spain) must be heard; or in case of demolition that the civil authorities cannot proceed without the mosques first being stripped of their sacred character by the competent Muslim religious authorities unless in cases of an emergency or imminent danger.

Ley 26/1992, de 10 de noviembre, por la que se aprueba el Acuerdo de Cooperación del Estado con la Comisión Islámica de España

Artículo 2.2:
Los lugares de culto de las Comunidades Islámicas miembros de la «Comisión Islámica de España» gozan de inviolabilidad en los términos establecidos por las Leyes. En caso de expropiación forzosa, deberá ser oída previamente la «Comisión Islámica de España», y no podrán ser demolidos sin ser previamente privados de su carácter sagrado, con excepción de los casos previstos en las Leyes, por razones de urgencia

o peligro. También quedarán exceptuados de la ocupación temporal e imposición de servidumbres en los términos previstos en el artículo 119 de la Ley de Expropiación Forzosa

This law does not explain the term inviolability; it only says "in terms established by the law". So it is considered that inviolability has the constitutional meaning of inviolability of the home (art. 18.2 Spanish Constitution).

Constitución Española
Artículo 18.2:
El domicilio es inviolable. Ninguna entrada o registro podrá hacerse en él sin consentimiento del titular o resolución judicial, salvo en caso de flagrante delito

Initially, registration in the Register of Religious Entities was optional when opening a religious centre, although it was considered convenient for enjoying the rights established in the Cooperation Agreement, such as, for example, tax benefits for places of worship. But since 2013 (in accordance with Law 27/2013, of 27 December 2013, on the rationalisation and sustainability of the local administration), it has been established that "for the opening of places of worship, churches, denominations or religious communities should prove their legal personality by certificate of the Registry of Religious Entities ..."

Ley 27/2013, de 27 de diciembre, de racionalización y sostenibilidad de la Administración Local
BOE» núm. 312, de 30 de diciembre de 2013,
Disposición adicional decimoséptima. Apertura de lugares de culto.
Para la apertura de lugares de culto las iglesias, confesiones o comunidades religiosas deberán acreditar su personalidad jurídica civil mediante certificado del Registro de Entidades Religiosas, emitido al efecto, en el que constará la ubicación del lugar de culto que se pretenda constituir. Obtenida esa certificación, su tramitación se ajustará a lo dispuesto en el artículo 84.1.c) de la Ley 7/1985, de 2 de abril, reguladora de las Bases del Régimen Local, sin perjuicio de recabar la licencia urbanística que corresponda.

The spatial integration of Islam in Spanish society manifests a strong contrast between the great Islamic cultural centres with their clearly identifiable architectural form especially their minarets, and prayer rooms in garages that were opened at the initiative of small immigrant communities without any symbols that might identify them as religious centres in the public space. The paradox is that while these well-known centres are part of the urban landscape of the cities where they are located, it is the prayer rooms that, despite their invisibility, are the targets of social opposition to their location.

The first Muslim centres that were opened in Spain in modern times[1] were built in the early 1980s and sponsored by several Muslim countries (such as Saudi Arabia). The Omar ibn al-Jattab Mosque, or Islamic Cultural Centre of Madrid (popularly known as the mosque of the M-30, a highway that circles Madrid), inaugurated in 1992, was the largest mosque in Europe until the inauguration in 1997 of the Islamic Centre in Rome. Starting in the 1990s, other large centres were opened, especially in Andalusia.

Apart from these unique spaces, which are the result of diplomatic initiatives promoted by Muslim countries, there is a large network of centres of worship spread throughout Spanish territory, with a very diverse typology of spaces: from garages and warehouses to industrial buildings that are in peripheral urban areas. At a general level, these are spaces that show a discreet visibility, and that on occasions have been the object of protests against their opening by the residents of the neighbourhoods in which they are located.[2]

4.2 The Catalan Places of Worship Law

The Autonomous Regions and Municipalities are responsible for territorial planning and therefore also for the building regulations of mosques. Building and renovations are subject to urban planning rules relating both to planning (reserve of land in the General Plans of Urban Planning) and to administrative licences.[3]

Catalonia was the first Autonomous Region to pass a law regarding places of worship (Law 16/2009, 22 July 22).[4] The Parliament of Catalonia passed the Places of Worship Law on 2009 with three objectives: to facilitate the exercise of the right to religious freedom, to support local councils in guaran-

1 During the Protectorate of Northern Morocco (1912–1956), the Spanish colonial administration built mosques, prayer halls and other Islamic religious buildings. The two main mosques of Ceuta and Melilla, the mosque Sidi M'barik and the mosque on the street Garcia Cabrelles, respectively, are good examples of this.

2 See Moreras (2009) and Astor (2017).

3 See Rodríguez Blanco (2000: 195–196).

4 The text of the law can be consulted here: http://justicia.gencat.cat/ca/ambits/afers-religiosos/serveis/centres-de-culte/index.html#googtrans(ca|en).

teeing this right and to ensure adequate health and safety conditions in the premises used. To fulfil these goals the Law includes that local councils should provide land where religious use is permitted and municipal licences for the opening and use of places of worship if the legal requirements are fulfilled.

Ley 16/2009, de 22 de julio, de los centros de culto.
DOGC núm. 5432, de 30 de julio de 2009/ BOE núm. 198, de 17 de agosto de 2009

Artículo 4. Fijación de usos religiosos en los planes de ordenación urbanística municipal.
1. Los planes de ordenación urbanística municipal deben prever suelos con la calificación de sistema de equipamiento comunitario donde se admitan los usos de carácter religioso de nueva implantación, de acuerdo con las necesidades y disponibilidades de los municipios. A tal efecto, deben tenerse en cuenta la información y los datos contenidos en estos planes.
2. Las necesidades y disponibilidades municipales no pueden determinarse en ningún caso en función de criterios que puedan comportar algún tipo de discriminación por motivos religiosos o de convicción.

Artículo 5. Asignación de uso religioso y participación de las confesiones.
1. Para la asignación del uso religioso a los suelos calificados de equipamiento comunitario, debe aplicarse la legislación urbanística vigente.
2. Las iglesias, las confesiones y las comunidades religiosas, con la finalidad de que se conozcan y puedan preverse las necesidades existentes en relación con la construcción de lugares de culto, tienen derecho a participar en el proceso de formulación del planeamiento urbanístico, mediante los canales que establecen los programas de participación ciudadana de los planes de ordenación urbanística municipal y con la participación en los plazos de información pública establecidos por la legislación urbanística para la tramitación del planeamiento urbanístico.
Artículo 6. Uso esporádico de equipamientos o espacios de titularidad pública con finalidades religiosas.
Las administraciones públicas deben garantizar a las iglesias, las confesiones y las comunidades religiosas un trato igualitario y no discriminatorio en las cesiones y autorizaciones de uso de equipamientos y espacios públicos, de uso privativo del dominio público, de ocupación temporal de la vía pública o de uso de bienes patrimoniales para llevar a cabo actividades esporádicas de carácter religioso.

On 20 July 2010 the Catalan Government passed the decree implementing in Catalonia the Places of Worship Law which establishes the technical and material conditions required for the opening of places of worship, such as accessibility conditions and car parks.

Decreto 94/2010, de 20 de julio, de desarrollo de la Ley 16/2009, de 22 de julio, de los centros de culto.
DOGC núm 5676 de 22 de julio de 2010

Artículo 7. Criterios y condiciones urbanísticas de accesibilidad y aparcamiento aplicables en los centros de culto de gran capacidad.

Para la implantación de centros de culto en suelos calificados de equipamientos comunitarios, que tengan una superficie construida superior a mil metros cuadrados o un aforo previsto para más de quinientas personas, tanto en edificios de nueva planta como en edificios existentes, la documentación del plan especial urbanístico de concreción del uso y de establecimiento de las condiciones de ordenación y de edificación del equipamiento, tiene que incorporar una justificación sobre la idoneidad y conveniencia de la implantación del nuevo centro. Asimismo, tiene que contener un estudio de la movilidad generada y de las necesidades de plazas de aparcamiento de la nueva implantación y el planteamiento de las soluciones contempladas con el fin de garantizar la corrección de los posibles déficits generados.

On 27 January 2014 the Catalan Government decided that places of worship which did not have yet a licence had to conform to the regulation by 2020.

The urban regulations come basically from the Autonomous Regions (17 in Spain), although there is some State-level legislation.[5] Both State and regional laws recognise that the General Urban Planning Plans must reserve areas for centres at the service of the community that are called *emplazamientos* or "community facilities". And these areas dedicated to public interest, in accordance with those norms, have to include "reserved places for places of worship" and cemeteries. Once the urban plan has been approved by the city council, the corporation can transfer some land to the Islamic communities by way of sale or free transfer for a certain period (leasehold contract).

5 See Castro-Uriarte (2021).

The fact that a religious confession has the right to ask for a piece of land to build a mosque in the urban plan does not imply that the municipality must grant it automatically. The municipalities, when they design their urban planning, have certain discretionary powers to decide, although this does not mean either absolute or unlimited power. The municipal public authorities must always act in compliance with the urban regulations and legal system. And if the request for land to build a temple is a manifestation of a fundamental right (religious freedom), and if, in addition, it can be a lever for integration and social cohesion, if the local administration decides to deny the request for land reservation, that denial shall be clearly justified in the Planning Report.

Licences are administrative acts, by virtue of which, transformation of lands or spaces provided for in the general urban plan is authorised once it has been verified by the local Administration that the place of worship (mosque or prayer house) will respect both the requirements of the public interest and urban planning standards. There are no specific regulations on the establishment and renovation of religious buildings. Some municipalities used to apply to the denominations that wanted to renovate an apartment to transform it into a mosque specific licences for mercantile or industrial establishments. The Supreme Court recalled that, not being denominations commercial or industrial establishments, municipalities cannot apply to them the regulations aimed to those entities.[6] Nowadays, the procedure that some municipalities use to verify that a place that is going to be used as a place of worship complies with the minimum legal requirements of being safe, healthy and quiet enough is either the issue of specific licences or, above all, by way of "prior communication" or "responsible declaration".

> Ley 39/2015, de 1 de octubre, del Procedimiento Administrativo Común de las Administraciones Públicas
> BOE núm. 236, de 02/10/2015
> Artículo 69: Declaración responsable y comunicación.
> 1. "[…] se entenderá por declaración responsable el documento suscrito por un interesado en el que éste manifiesta, bajo su responsabilidad, que cumple con los requisitos establecidos en la normativa vigente para obtener el reconocimiento de un derecho o facultad o para su ejercicio, que dispone de la documentación que así lo acredita, que la pondrá a disposición de la Administración cuando le sea requerida, y que se compromete

6 Vid. STS de 24 de junio de 1988 (RAJ 4724).

> a mantener el cumplimiento de las anteriores obligaciones durante el período de tiempo inherente a dicho reconocimiento o ejercicio
> Los requisitos a los que se refiere el párrafo anterior deberán estar recogidos de manera expresa, clara y precisa en la correspondiente declaración responsable. Las Administraciones podrán requerir en cualquier momento que se aporte la documentación que acredite el cumplimiento de los mencionados requisitos y el interesado deberá aportarla.
> 2. A los efectos de esta Ley, se entenderá por comunicación aquel documento mediante el que los interesados ponen en conocimiento de la Administración Pública competente sus datos identificativos o cualquier otro dato relevante para el inicio de una actividad o el ejercicio de un derecho.
> 3. Las declaraciones responsables y las comunicaciones permitirán, el reconocimiento o ejercicio de un derecho o bien el inicio de una actividad, desde el día de su presentación, sin perjuicio de las facultades de comprobación, control e inspección que tengan atribuidas las Administraciones Públicas. […]"

So, if a Muslim community wants to transform a building into a place of worship, it should be enough to present to the municipal authorities document which includes their identifying data (certificate issued by the Registry of Religious Entities of its religious nature), their wish to open a place of worship in that specific place, and a declaration of intent to perform their religious activities from that day on. Of course, the Municipality can verify at any moment the fulfilment of that declaration.

CHAPTER 5

Status of Imams

In the text of the 1992 Cooperation Agreement signed with the Islamic Commission of Spain, the only reference to a figure of religious authority is to the imam, who is recognised as having a series of functions of worship and religious care.

> Ley 26/1992, de 10 de noviembre, por la que se aprueba el Acuerdo de Cooperación del Estado con la Comisión Islámica de España
>
> Artículo 3.1:
> A los efectos legales, son dirigentes religiosos islámicos e Imanes de las comunidades islámicas las personas físicas dedicadas, con carácter estable, a la dirección de las Comunidades a que se refiere el artículo 1 del presente Acuerdo, a la dirección de la oración, formación y asistencia religiosa islámica y acrediten el cumplimiento de estos requisitos mediante certificación expedida por la Comunidad a que pertenezcan, con la conformidad de la Comisión Islámica de España.

The respective texts signed with Protestants and Jews in this same year also referred to their religious authority figures, so a process of equalisation between all of them was established from the legal point of view, with respect to both their rights and their duties. There is a tacit comparison of these figures with respect to those that are defined on the model of the Catholic priesthood, which is a legal fiction. The model derived from the framework of legal and institutional relations with the Catholic Church has served as inspiration to broaden this framework of recognition in relation to the other three monotheistic minorities. Perhaps Islam, due to its own organisational tradition around religious authority, has raised the most doubts in its adjustment to this model.

Muslim representatives may argue that an imam is not a priest, or that in Islam there is no hierarchical institution as in the Catholic Church. But this did not prevent them during the negotiations prior to the Cooperation Agreement[1] from proposing the recognition of imams according to a logic that insists more on the position than on the function, as well as on their location within a more

1 Fernández-Coronado, (1995).

or less vertically structured organisation chart of Islam in Europe. The analysis of the third article of the Cooperation Agreement clearly shows this argument.

In the first place, the article establishes a comparison between religious leaders and imams which would not be inconsistent with the role of religious guide that these figures are expected to fulfil, since the text then indicates as one of their main tasks the direction of Islamic communities. In fact, the incorporation of a principle of community leadership was introduced in the preliminary draft of the final text of the Agreement, presented by the Ministry of Justice almost at the end of the negotiations held with the representatives of the FEERI and the UCIDE, in a meeting on 20 February 1992, after having analysed the two projects presented by both federations in January and June 1991, respectively. In these two projects the functions of imams or religious leaders were limited to activities of worship, education and religious assistance, but not to the leadership of their communities. This introduces an element of confusion between a community leadership and a doctrinal guide, which today reinforces the widely accepted idea that imams are the figures that represent the leadership in these groups.[2]

Secondly, the text of the article emphasises that these religious leaders and imams have to carry out their work in a consistent manner. The representatives of the FEERI presented to the Advisory Commission on Religious Freedom a series of amendments to and comments on the preliminary draft presented by the Ministry of Justice on 20 October 1991. One of them tried to replace the notion of "consistent manner" of these personnel by one of "habitual dedication", arguing that the task of imams was more a function than a position. The Advisory Commission at its meeting on 13 December 1991 dismissed this appeal for reasons of legal certainty. This article reinforces the bureaucratisation of the figure of the imam, by understanding not only that there cannot be an imam if he is not attached to a specific mosque, but also that a series of responsibilities of worship and community leadership falls on him which contribute to equating him with other ministers of worship.

These religious functions, thirdly, are expressed in the activities of worship, training and assistance. In fact, and as Ramírez Navalón[3] recalls, these three functions are globally defined by the State, since they can encapsulate the reli-

2 In fact, by this distinction the representatives of the FEERI wanted to achieve the opposite objective: the ability clearly to distinguish between what would be a properly religious leadership (the imams) and what would be an associative or community leadership, which would also recognise this leadership of the collective in a non-doctrinal key.

3 Ramírez Navalón (1994: 140).

gious purposes of the confessions that thus may be worthy of their recognition. Each denomination is the entity that defines the functions of its ministers of worship. The text of the article makes explicit reference to the primary function of an imam, such as the leadership of the community during prayer. In the two projects presented by the two federations, as well as in the successive comments to the preliminary projects presented by the Ministry, the replacement of this explicit reference by a more generic one such as "worship functions" was requested but was finally not accepted by the State negotiators.

Fourthly, at the end of the article reference is made to the accreditation necessary to exercise these religious functions. This is not given to someone who demonstrates competence in doctrinal matters, in accordance with some standard requirements (such as, for example, having completed formal studies or having an official certification), but is simply based on the certification made by the same community with the acquiescence or endorsement of the Islamic Commission. Thus, the decision is left in the hands of those responsible for the community itself, who can accept that person's competence by referencing other criteria, not necessarily curricular ones from a perspective of Western regulated education. It is interesting to mention the proposal that included the draft Agreement presented by the UCIDE, which requested that appointments and removals of imams at the head of the different communities be registered in the Registry of Religious Entities, which was not accepted then.

The most decisive element, however, that derives from this article is the fact that the recognition of imams and religious leaders must be linked to an Islamic religious entity, registered in the Register of Religious Entities of the Ministry of Justice and attached to any of the federations under the umbrella of the Islamic Commission of Spain.

The current regulation of the Registry of Religious Entities allow the registration of ministers of worship, that is, also that of imams (article 3) and adds that this registration is mandatory when the imam performs religious acts with civil effects, such as marriage (article 18).

Real Decreto 594/2015, de 3 de julio, por el que se regula el Registro de Entidades Religiosas
BOE núm. 183, de 1 de agosto de 2015,

Artículo 3. "Actos con acceso al Registro.
Tendrán acceso al Registro, de acuerdo con el procedimiento que se establece en este real decreto, los siguientes actos: (...) g) Los ministros de culto.

Capítulo V Anotación de la condición de ministro de culto
Artículo 18. Solicitud de anotación y documentación que debe aportarse.
1. Las entidades religiosas inscritas podrán anotar en el Registro de Entidades Religiosas a sus ministros de culto que ostenten residencia legal en España. En todo caso, deberán anotarse aquellos ministros de culto que estén habilitados para realizar actos religiosos con efectos civiles.
2. Para efectuar dicha anotación los representantes legales de la entidad deberán presentar certificación de la Iglesia, Confesión o Comunidad religiosa a que pertenezcan que acredite tal condición y, si lo hubiere, el visto bueno del órgano supremo en España de la entidad conforme a sus propias normas. Cuando se trate de entidades integradas en una Federación inscrita, será necesario también el visto bueno del órgano competente de la respectiva Federación cuando así se disponga en sus estatutos, sin perjuicio de lo dispuesto en los Acuerdos de Cooperación con el Estado respecto de las entidades o Federaciones firmantes de los mismos.
3. Las entidades deberán comunicar al Registro las bajas de sus ministros de culto y solicitar su cancelación en el plazo de un mes desde que la baja tuvo lugar.
4. La resolución de la anotación y cancelación de ministros de culto de las entidades religiosas se dictará por el titular de la Subdirección General de Relaciones con las Confesiones. Transcurrido el plazo de tres meses a contar desde la fecha en que la solicitud haya tenido entrada en cualquiera de los Registros del Ministerio de Justicia, si no se hubiese dictado y notificado resolución, se entenderá estimada, de acuerdo con lo dispuesto en el artículo 43 de la Ley 30/1992, de 26 de noviembre.
5. La certificación registral de la anotación del ministro de culto será prueba suficiente para acreditar dicha cualidad. El certificado tendrá una vigencia de dos años pudiendo ser renovado por iguales periodos.

However, the Law passing the Cooperation Agreement requires only that Islamic marriage must be celebrated before an imam who meets the requirements of stability and certification by his community, in the terms established in its article 3, and this article does not require that the imam be registered in the RRE. Thus, an Islamic marriage would not cease to be valid because the imam before whom it is celebrated was not registered in the RRE.

Islamic communities have the right to appoint any imam they wish, since religious confessions have autonomy to appoint their ministers of worship.

Ley Orgánica 7/1980, de 5 de julio, de Libertad Religiosa

Artículo 6.1: Las Iglesias, Confesiones y Comunidades religiosas inscritas tendrán plena autonomía y podrán establecer sus propias normas de organización, régimen interno y régimen de su personal.

In principle, the legal relationship that unites an imam with his community is not an employment relationship since imams offer their functions to a religious community and not to an ordinary employer. In legal terms, they are not workers. But the law allows imams who receive a salary from their religious communities to be equated with paid workers and to be integrated into the Social Security system. However, in order to obtain the benefit of been included in the Social Security system in conditions very similar to those of ordinary workers, the law requires that they offer their religious services with a certain stability.

Even though the text of the AC recognises imams as people dedicated in a stable manner to the tasks of worship and religious care, this stability is broadly interpreted. It is contrasted with an informal situation, but, at the same time, it does not imply exclusivity. In fact, in Spain many imams provide religious service as volunteers or combine that function with other work in order to supplement the modest salary that Muslim communities with few financial resources can offer.

Thus, imams that meet the requirements defined in article 3 of the AC (see below) will be covered by the Social Security system in which they have similar status to that of employees. Like other ministers of worship, imams are not legally workers because they work, on non-profit-making terms, not really for a regular employer but for the religious community to which they belong. Even so, their respective Islamic communities assume the rights and obligations of employers, as laid down in the fifth article of the AC.

Ley 26/1992, de 10 de noviembre, por la que se aprueba el Acuerdo de Cooperación del Estado con la Comisión Islámica de España

Artículo 5:
De acuerdo con lo dispuesto en el artículo 1 del Real Decreto 2398/1977, de 27 de agosto, las personas que reúnan los requisitos expresados en el número 1 del artículo 3 del presente Convenio, quedarán incluidos en el Régimen General de la Seguridad Social, asimilados a trabajadores por cuenta ajena. Las Comunidades Islámicas respectivas asumirán los derechos y obligaciones establecidas para los empresarios en el Régimen General de la Seguridad Social".

This article was later expanded by Royal Decree 176 of 10 February 2006 in relation to the terms and conditions of inclusion in the social security system of religious leaders and imams of the Islamic communities that are members of the Islamic Commission of Spain. As established by this royal decree, Muslim communities must notify the General Treasury of Social Security of the hiring of the imam as a "worker" at the service of the community for him to be registered in the Social Security System. Similarly, if he is dismissed as an imam in a mosque, those who hired him must notify the Treasury of his dismissal. Imams who receive salaries from their communities are obliged to pay Social Security levies (workers' contributions), and their Islamic communities must also contribute as entrepreneurs (employers' contributions). Based on these assumptions, imams receive the benefits of the Social Security System with the only exception of unemployment protection.

Real Decreto 176/2006, de 10 de febrero, sobre términos y condiciones de inclusión en el Régimen General de la Seguridad Social de los dirigentes religiosos e imames de las comunidades integradas en la Comisión Islámica de España
BOE núm. 42, de 18 de febrero de 2006

Artículo 1:
La acción protectora, por lo que respecta al colectivo al que se refiere el artículo anterior, será la correspondiente al Régimen General de la Seguridad Social, con la única exclusión de la protección por desempleo. 2. Las contingencias de enfermedad y accidente, cualquiera que sea su origen, se considerarán, en todo caso, como común y no laboral, respectivamente, siéndoles de aplicación el régimen jurídico.

Some imams, such as those mentioned in article 9 of the AC, provide their religious services in public facilities, for example, in prisons, hospitals or any other social facilities that depend on the State.

Ley 26/1992, de 10 de noviembre, por la que se aprueba el Acuerdo de Cooperación del Estado con la Comisión Islámica de España

Artículo 9.1:
Se garantiza el ejercicio del derecho a la asistencia religiosa de los internados en centros o establecimientos penitenciarios, hospitalarios, asistenciales u otros análogos del sector público, proporcionada por los Imanes o personas designadas por las Comunidades, que deberán ser autoriza-

dos por los organismos administrativos competentes. Las direcciones de los centros o establecimientos públicos estarán obligadas a transmitir a la Comunidad Islámica correspondiente las solicitudes de asistencia religiosa recibidas de los internos o de sus familiares, si los propios interesados no estuvieran en condiciones de hacerlo. La asistencia religiosa prevista en este artículo comprenderá la que se dispense a los moribundos, así como las honras fúnebres del rito islámico.

In these cases, the legal relationship that binds those imams to those public institutions is different because the employer in these cases is the State, not the Islamic community. The contract binds them to the State through a regular labour or administrative contract.

Bearing in mind that a significant number of the imams who work in Spain are foreigners, the question then arises of the residence permits that these religious personnel must obtain. The current Organic Law on Immigration (4/2000, amended by 8/2000 and 14/2003) refers to an exemption from the work permit requirements for these religious specialists, although in the regulations for the execution of the law (Royal Decree 864/2001, of 20 July 2001) this exemption is specified in more detail. Two other conditions have been added to the requirements: to belong to a registered confession and to develop properly religious tasks, which requires having certification of their religious training, and not developing paid activities.

Ley Orgánica 4/2000, de 11 de enero, sobre derechos y libertades de los extranjeros en España y su integración social.
BOE núm. 10, de 12/01/2000

Artículo 41. Excepciones al permiso de trabajo: No será necesaria la obtención de permiso de trabajo para el ejercicio de las actividades siguientes: [...] h) los ministros, religiosos o representantes de las diferentes iglesias y confesiones, debidamente inscritas en el Registro de Entidades Religiosas, en tanto limiten su actividad a funciones estrictamente religiosas

Real Decreto 864/2001, de 20 de julio, por el que se aprueba el Reglamento de ejecución de la Ley Orgánica 4/2000, de 11 de enero, sobre derechos y libertades de los extranjeros en España y su integración social, reformada por Ley Orgánica 8/2000, de 22 de diciembre
BOE núm. 174, de 21 de julio de 2001

> Artículo 68. Excepciones al permiso de trabajo
> 1. Serán exceptuadas de la obligación de obtener permiso de trabajo para el ejercicio de las actividades que motivan la excepción las personas que, estando incluidas en el artículo 41 de la Ley Orgánica 4/2000, reformada por Ley Orgánica 8/2000, cumplan las condiciones que se establecen en el presente artículo: [...]
> h) Ministros, religiosos o representantes de las diferentes iglesias y confesiones. Tendrán esta consideración las personas en quienes concurran los siguientes requisitos:
> 1. Que pertenezcan a una iglesia o confesión que figure debidamente inscrita en el Registro de Entidades Religiosas del Ministerio de Justicia.
> 2. Que tengan, previa verificación del Ministerio de Justicia, la condición de ministros del culto, religiosos o representantes de las distintas iglesias y confesiones, habiendo profesado o realizado los estudios requeridos para ello, según las normas internas de las mismas y se hallen investidos y facultados para el ejercicio de su ministerio o para la administración de los sacramentos.
> 3. Que las actividades a desarrollar en España sean estrictamente religiosas, por estar relacionadas de forma directa con el culto, ser meramente contemplativas o respondan a la misión propia y característica de la Orden.
> 4. Que no pretendan desarrollar actividades retribuidas, aunque se correspondan con la misión de su iglesia o confesión, ni sean personas vinculadas con una orden, confesión o religión que aún no hayan profesado, aunque temporalmente realicen actividades de carácter pastoral, así como los estudiantes, postulantes, novicios y asociados, aunque lleven a cabo actividades encaminadas a adquirir posteriormente la condición de ministros, sacerdotes o religiosos, o realicen una actividad o servicio temporal en cumplimiento de sus estatutos religiosos.

This same legal framework allows foreign imams who are temporally in Spain to carry out religious work, for example during the month of Ramadan, not to need work permits (although they still need residence permits) if they limit their activity strictly to religious functions.

Imams and Islamic religious leaders are entitled to the right to confidentiality. As set out in article 3.2 of the AC with CIE, under no circumstances may religious leaders and imams be forced to reveal information disclosed to them in the exercise of their duties as prayer leaders, preachers and spiritual counsellors by virtue of the privilege of confidentiality conferred on them by law.

> Ley 26/1992, de 10 de noviembre, por la que se aprueba el Acuerdo de Cooperación del Estado con la Comisión Islámica de España
>
> Artículo 3.2: En ningún caso las personas expresadas en el número anterior [dirigentes religiosos islámicos e Imanes] estarán obligadas a declarar sobre hechos que les hayan sido revelados en el ejercicio de sus funciones de culto o de asistencia religiosa islámica, en los términos legalmente establecidos para el secreto profesional.

This is an exception to the duty of every citizen to collaborate with the judicial authorities in the conduct of judicial processes. It has a direct parallel with the secrecy of the confessional that is recognised for Catholic priests in the Agreement signed by the State and the Holy See on 28 July 1976. Given that in Islam there is no institution equivalent to the Catholic confessional, exegetical problems may arise regarding the scope of this article.

CHAPTER 6

Burial and Cemeteries

Cemeteries are not properly places of worship, but they are definitely places of public service. The current State legislation (Law 49/1978 of burials in the municipal cemeteries) was approved shortly before the Constitution came into force. This legislation put an end to previous discrimination for religious reasons within cemeteries, proclaiming the freedom of rites within it. For some years now concrete proposals have been made to ensure that people can be buried according to their own religious and spiritual consciences.[1]

Ley 49/1978, de 3 de noviembre, de enterramientos en cementerios municipales BOE (07 de noviembre de 1978)

Artículo 1:
Los Ayuntamientos están obligados a que los enterramientos que se efectúen en sus cementerios se realicen sin discriminación alguna por razones de religión ni por cualesquiera otras.

Disposición Transitoria Primera
En el plazo de un año a partir de la vigencia de la presente Ley deberá procederse, en aquellos cementerios municipales donde hubiera lugares separados destinados a los que hasta ahora se denominaban cementerios civiles, a restablecer la comunicación con el resto del cementerio.

The Religious Freedom Act later proclaimed the right of individuals "to receive a dignified burial".[2] Law 7/1985 on Bases of Local Government emphasised that municipalities were the competent authorities in the matter of cemeteries (articles 25 and 26), and Law 14/1986 on General Health insists that it is the municipalities that must ensure sanitary conditions and provide mortuary police (article 42.2. e).

Ley 7/1985, de 2 de abril, Reguladora de las Bases del Régimen Local.
BOE núm. 80, de 03 de abril de 1985

1 See Moreras-Tarrés (2013a) and Ministerio de Justicia (2019).

2 See chapter 1.1.1.

Artículo 25.
[…]
2. El Municipio ejercerá en todo caso como competencias propias […] en las siguientes materias: […]
k) Cementerios y actividades funerarias. […]

Artículo 26. 1. Los Municipios deberán prestar […] los servicios siguientes:
a) En todos los Municipios: alumbrado público, cementerio, recogida de residuos, limpieza viaria, abastecimiento domiciliario de agua potable, alcantarillado, acceso a los núcleos de población y pavimentación de las vías públicas. […]

Ley 14/1986, de 25 de abril, General de Sanidad.
«BOE» núm. 102, de 29 de abril de 1986

Artículo cuarenta y dos. […]
3. No obstante, los Ayuntamientos, sin perjuicio de las competencias de las demás Administraciones Públicas, tendrán las siguientes responsabilidades mínimas en relación al obligado cumplimiento de las normas y planes sanitarios […]
e) Control sanitario de los cementerios y policía sanitaria mortuoria.

Cemeteries can be public or private. The municipal authorities exercise their powers over all of them, although to a lesser extent over private cemeteries, which are managed by the owners who can decide several issues, for example, about the people who can be buried in them, the rites followed, burial requirements etc. However, private cemeteries must also comply with the norms regarding public health, which are enforced by the municipalities.

The Cooperation Agreement of 1992 between the State and the CIE recognised in article 2.5 that the Islamic communities integrated in the CIE are entitled to be granted plots reserved for Muslim burials in municipal cemeteries, and to own their own Islamic cemeteries.

Ley 26/1992, de 10 de noviembre, por la que se aprueba el Acuerdo de Cooperación del Estado con la Comisión Islámica de España

Artículo 2.5
Los cementerios islámicos gozarán de los beneficios legales que establece el número 2 de este mismo artículo para los lugares de culto.

Se reconoce a las Comunidades Islámicas, pertenecientes a la «Comisión Islámica de España», el derecho a la concesión de parcelas reservadas para los enterramientos islámicos en los cementerios municipales, así como el derecho a poseer cementerios islámicos propios.
Se adoptarán las medidas oportunas para la observancia de las reglas tradicionales islámicas, relativas a inhumaciones, sepulturas y ritos funerarios que se realizarán con intervención de la Comunidad Islámica local.
Se reconoce el derecho a trasladar a los cementerios pertenecientes a las Comunidades Islámicas los cuerpos de los difuntos musulmanes, tanto los actualmente inhumados en cementerios municipales como los de aquéllos cuyo fallecimiento se produzca en localidad en la que no exista cementerio islámico, con sujeción a lo dispuesto en la legislación de régimen local y de sanidad

6.1 Accommodating Muslim Funeral Rites

Some Islamic funeral rites, such as burial in tombs above ground and with the deceased's head facing Mecca, do not necessarily pose problems. Likewise, the fact of burying the Muslim deceased in a different area from the deceased of other religious traditions has been accepted directly by the different managers of municipal cemeteries without any problem.

More controversial has been the custom of transfer and burial of the corpse without a coffin. In national legislation (Decree 2263/1974), the Sanitary and Mortuary Police Regulation bans the coffinless transport, transfer and burial of corpses.

Decreto 2263/1974, de 20 de julio, por el que se aprueba el Reglamento de Policía Sanitaria Mortuoria
BOE núm. 197, de 17 de agosto de 1974

Artículo 9.
Se prohíbe la conducción, traslado y enterramiento de cadáveres sin el correspondiente féretro de las características que para cada caso se indican en este Reglamento.

This regulation is of subsidiary application to the specific regulations of the Autonomous Regions. But most Autonomous Regions have reproduced the obligation to bury in a coffin. However, some autonomous regions (such as Andalusia, Valencian Community Asturias, Castilla-León and the cities of

Ceuta and Melilla) have allowed burial without a coffin provided that there are guarantees that public health is not endangered.

Decreto 95/2001 de 3 de abril, sobre Regulaciones en materia de policía mortuoria. Junta de Andalucía (BOJA no. 50, 3-5-2001).
Artículo 21: "En aquellos casos en que, por razones de confesionalidad, así se solicite y se autorice por el Ayuntamiento, (...), podrá eximirse del uso de féretro para enterramiento, aunque no para la conducción".

Another problematic element in the recognition of Islamic burial traditions is burying the corpse within 24 hours of the death in accordance with Islamic tradition. In EU countries, to ensure certainty of death, a longer period (between 24 and 36 hours) is generally required between death and burial. In Spain, the national funeral regulations require that, after confirmation of death by a doctor, corpses must remain in the funeral home for 24 to 48 hours (article 15.1).

Decreto 2263/1974, de 20 de julio, por el que se aprueba el Reglamento de Policía Sanitaria Mortuoria

Artículo 15.
Los cadáveres permanecerán en el domicilio mortuorio hasta después de la confirmación de la defunción por el médico adscrito al Registro Civil. Esta permanencia no podrá ser inferior, con carácter general, a las veinticuatro horas, ni exceder de cuarenta y ocho horas desde la del fallecimiento.

But this issue remains vague, given that repatriation of the body of a Muslim deceased acquires an important relevance. It is estimated that some Muslim groups (such as Moroccans and Senegalese) repatriate 90 per cent of their deceased to their region of origin.[3] Repatriating a corpse is a complex process that usually takes between ten and 15 days, though with delays it can take up to a month. The international transport of dead bodies is regulated by the multilateral Agreement on the Transfer of Corpses (1973). The Spanish law requires that any corpse that is not to be buried within 48 hours following death must be embalmed, which means that every repatriated corpse is embalmed. International regulations also require that corpses travel inside hermetically sealed coffins. Funeral companies in Spain have adapted their procedures to take care

3 See Moreras-Solé (2019).

of this process. In accordance with diplomatic law, consulates take responsibility for the bureaucratic procedures arising from the repatriation of their nationals in the event of their death. Consular delegations provide the documentation required to identify the deceased and determine their region of origin. Consulates also recommend taking out family repatriation insurance, but there are still people without insurance coverage whose repatriation in the event of death is covered by Muslim communities acting together. Therefore, the increasingly prevalent response of Moroccan and Senegalese groups to the imperative of repatriation as the preferred option is indicative of the progressive consolidation of their communities' organisational structures.

Due to the pandemic caused by covid-19, repatriations from Spain had to be cancelled during the first half of 2020. This generated the need to open new plots reserved for Muslim burials in various Spanish locations.[4]

6.2 Islamic Cemeteries

For years the Islamic Commission of Spain has demanded that each Spanish province or region have a Muslim cemetery for the burial of the deceased Muslims who reside in that territory. The need to provide space in municipal cemeteries for the Muslim population has arisen recently with the increasing settlement of Muslims in Spain.[5] Hitherto, the existing cemeteries were either those in Ceuta and Melilla (whose Muslim cemeteries were managed by the different communities in the two cities), historical cemeteries (like those in Seville and Granada, opened in 1936 by the Franco regime to bury Moroccan troops who fought in the Civil War) or cemeteries that belonged to the governments of Muslim countries and were used for their employees or citizens (such as the cemetery of Griñón in Madrid, which has now reached capacity). In Andalusia, various groups of Spanish Muslims have always called for spaces, which were ultimately acquired and maintained by personal initiatives; they did not always provide appropriate conditions and are filling rapidly. Since 1992, the Cooperation Agreement has recognised the right of Muslims to make use of sites in public cemeteries. There are currently a total of 28 areas reserved in municipal cemeteries for burials according to Islamic rituals, as well as three private Muslim cemeteries.

4 See Martínez-Torrón (2020) and Rodrigo Lara (2020).

5 See Moreras-Tarrés (2013b).

CHAPTER 7

Education and Schools

The Spanish Education System is based on three models of school establishments (public schools, private schools with partial funding from the State, *concertados*, and private schools without State funding). As yet there are neither private nor *concertados* Islamic schools within the Spanish education system. However, Muslim pupils are entitled, upon request, to receive Islamic religious instruction in public schools, at pre-school, primary and secondary levels. Teachers of Islam in public schools are paid by the State if they have at least ten students per class. This principle is based on the right recognised by the Spanish Constitution to choose religious education based on the convictions of the parents: "The public authorities guarantee the right of parents to ensure that their children receive religious and moral instruction in accordance with their own convictions" (CE article 27.3).

Constitución Española de 1978

Artículo 27.3:
Los poderes públicos garantizan el derecho que asiste a los padres para que sus hijos reciban la formación religiosa y moral que esté de acuerdo con sus propias convicciones.

It cannot be deduced from these words that the Constitution obliges public schools to teach religious education. This right of parents can be guaranteed either at school, at home or somewhere else. However, by virtue of the Teaching Agreement on Education signed by the Spanish State and the Holy See in 1979, religious education must be integrated into the curricula of primary, secondary and primary schools.

Instrumento de Ratificación del Acuerdo entre el Estado español y la Santa Sede sobre Enseñanza y asuntos culturales, firmado en Ciudad del Vaticano el 3 de enero de 1979
BOE» núm. 300, de 15 de diciembre de 1979

Artículo II
Los planes educativos en los niveles de Educación Preescolar, de Educación General Básica (EGB) y de Bachillerato Unificado Polivalente (BUP)

y Grados de Formación Profesional correspondientes a los alumnos de las mismas edades incluirán la enseñanza de la religión católica en todos los Centros de educación, en condiciones equiparables a las demás disciplinas fundamentales.
Por respeto a la libertad de conciencia, dicha enseñanza no tendrá carácter obligatorio para los alumnos. Se garantiza, sin embargo, el derecho a recibirla.
Las autoridades académicas adoptarán las medidas oportunas para que el hecho de recibir o no recibir la enseñanza religiosa no suponga discriminación alguna en la actividad escolar.
En los niveles de enseñanza mencionados, las autoridades académicas correspondientes permitirán que la jerarquía eclesiástica establezca, en las condiciones concretas que con ella se convenga, otras actividades complementarias de formación y asistencia religiosa.

The three Agreements signed in 1992 by the Spanish State with Muslims, Jews and Protestants tried to follow that same path. As for Muslims, article 10 of the Cooperation Agreement guarantees that in public and in publicly funded private schools, with the prior consent of parents and educators, Islamic religious education can be provided if it does not conflict with the religious ideology of the school. This article recognises among others five main aspects:

a) The right of students to receive Islamic religious education at pre-school, primary and secondary levels in public schools and State-subsidised private Islamic schools, but only upon request.
b) This education shall be provided by teachers appointed by communities that are members of the Islamic Commission of Spain, with the agreement of the federation to which they belong.
c) Islamic communities can organise religious education courses in public universities.
d) Islamic communities can create schools, private universities or imam training centres. The University Law (LO 4/2007, which modifies LOU) mandates the Government, in application of the Agreements of Cooperation of 1992, to regulate the recognition of university degrees for theological studies or training centres for imams, pastors and rabbis, but so far only the Catholic Church and the Protestants have official university degrees for theological studies.
e) The CIE has the responsibility to appoint teachers and prepare appropriate teaching materials, as well as the authority to organise courses and seminars on Islamic issues and to establish and run schools and centres for Islamic training.

Ley 26/1992, de 10 de noviembre, por la que se aprueba el Acuerdo de Cooperación del Estado con la Comisión Islámica de España

Artículo 10.
1. A fin de dar efectividad a lo dispuesto en el artículo 27.3 de la Constitución, así como en la Ley Orgánica 8/1985, de 3 de julio, Reguladora del Derecho a la Educación, y en la Ley Orgánica 1/1990, de 3 de octubre, de Ordenación General del Sistema Educativo, se garantiza a los alumnos musulmanes, a sus padres y a los órganos escolares de gobierno que lo soliciten, el ejercicio del derecho de los primeros a recibir enseñanza religiosa islámica en los centros docentes públicos y privados concertados, siempre que, en cuanto a estos últimos, el ejercicio de aquel derecho no entre en contradicción con el carácter propio del centro, en los niveles de educación infantil, educación primaria y educación secundaria.
2. La enseñanza religiosa islámica será impartida por profesores designados por las Comunidades pertenecientes a la «Comisión Islámica de España», con la conformidad de la Federación a que pertenezcan.
3. Los contenidos de la enseñanza religiosa islámica, así como los libros de texto relativos a la misma, serán proporcionados por las Comunidades respectivas, con la conformidad de la «Comisión Islámica de España».
4. Los centros docentes públicos y los privados concertados a que se hace referencia en el número 1 de este artículo, deberán facilitar los locales adecuados para el ejercicio del derecho que en este artículo se regula, sin que pueda perjudicar el desenvolvimiento de las actividades lectivas.
5. La «Comisión Islámica de España», así como sus Comunidades miembros, podrán organizar cursos de enseñanza religiosa en los centros universitarios públicos, pudiendo utilizar los locales y medios de los mismos, de acuerdo con las autoridades académicas.
6. La «Comisión Islámica de España», así como las Comunidades pertenecientes a la misma, podrán establecer y dirigir centros docentes de los niveles educativos que se mencionan en el número 1 de este artículo, así como Universidades y Centros de Formación Islámica, con sometimiento a la legislación general vigente en la materia.

The mixed commission composed of representatives of the Ministries of Justice and Education, as well as those of the CIE, was established in 1993 to implement Islamic religious education. The first step was to design a curriculum for it. The Islamic federations then existing (FEERI and UCIDE) presented different drafts, which again made the implementation of the Cooperation

Agreement difficult. Finally, on 18 January 1996, the *Curriculum for Islamic Education in Public and State-Assisted Schools* was approved and published in the Official Bulletin of State.[1]

The CIE and the Ministries of Justice and the Interior and of Education and Science signed the *Agreement on the Appointment and Remuneration of Persons Responsible for Islamic Religious Education in Primary and Secondary Schools* on 12 March 1996. This opened the door to the real possibility of Muslim students in public schools choosing to receive religious education.[2] This educational agreement was to serve to determine the public resources given by the State, which promised to finance classes of ten or more students.

Resolución de 23 de abril de 1996, de la Subsecretaría, por la que se dispone la publicación del Acuerdo del Consejo de Ministros, de 1 de marzo de 1996, y el Convenio sobre designación y régimen económico de las personas encargadas de la enseñanza religiosa evangélica, en los centros docentes públicos de educación primera y secundaria
BOE núm. 108, de 4 de mayo de 1996

Cláusula octava: [...] El Estado compensará económicamente a las comunidades islámicas por los servicios prestados por las personas que imparten enseñanza religiosa islámica en los correspondientes centros docentes públicos del Estado español, en los niveles de Educación Primaria y Educación Secundaria, optimizando las condiciones de impartición de dicha enseñanza, según lo que se establece a continuación: 1. Los alumnos y alumnas del mismo nivel educativo que, en un mismo centro, soliciten la enseñanza religiosa islámica, serán agrupados para recibir esta enseñanza. En este caso, el número de alumnos por grupo no será mayor que el establecido por la normativa vigente para la correspondiente etapa. 2. En el caso de que al aplicarse lo dispuesto en el apartado anterior, el grupo formado sea inferior a diez, se agruparán los alumnos y alumnas de diferentes niveles educativos de una misma etapa que, en un mismo centro,

1 ORDEN de 11 de enero de 1996 por la que se dispone la publicación de los currículums de Enseñanza Religiosa Islámica correspondientes a Educación Primaria, Educación Secundaria Obligatoria y Bachillerato. BOE núm. 16 de jueves 18 de enero de 1996.

2 Resolution of 23 April 1996 of the Undersecretary, which provides for the publication of the Agreement of the Council of Ministers, of 1 March 1996, and the Convention on the appointment and economic regime of persons in charge of Islamic religious education, in public educational centres of Primary and Secondary Education.

hubiesen solicitado recibir la enseñanza religiosa islámica. 3. La hora de clase de enseñanza religiosa islámica será compensada económicamente por el Estado cuando el número de alumnos a que se imparta, una vez aplicado lo acordado en los apartados 1 a 3 de esta cláusula, sea igual o superior a diez. El importe económico, por cada hora de enseñanza religiosa islámica, tendrá el mismo valor que la retribución real, por hora de clase, de cualquier materia impartida por un profesor interino del mismo nivel.

The Spanish government asked the CIE to prepare a list of qualified teachers. A pilot programme was set up and carried out during the 1996–1997 academic year in Ceuta and Melilla, where demand for the subject is much greater than in the rest of the country. In this first phase, the teachers were to be paid by the CIE on a provisional basis. The CIE accepted these conditions, having received the promise that the agreement would be implemented nationally in the following year with teachers being paid directly by the State.

The fact is that the demand to introduce Islamic education is added to the intense debate in Spanish society over the role of religion in schools. This could be one of the reasons explaining why, today, Islamic religious education has not been fully implemented in the Spanish educational system. Another reason has to do with the fact that in Spain this system is devolved in some autonomous regions, which has allowed each of them to show different degrees of willingness to develop this Islamic religious education.

Currently, no official data are available on the number of students who have received Islamic religious instruction. The only updated statistical information is that provided by the *Observatorio Andalusi* (UCIDE).[3] According to its latest report, in the 2019–2020 academic year a total of 326,359 Muslim students were counted, and there were only 80 accredited teachers to teach religious education. On the other hand, this report indicates that in the vast majority of autonomous communities Islamic religious education is being implemented, although in a basic and partial way, due to the evident lack of teachers: Andalusia is the community with most teachers (23), followed by Ceuta (14), Melilla (ten), Castilla y León (six), Aragón (five), País Vasco (five), La Rioja (five), Madrid (three), Comunidad Valenciana (three), Extremadura (three),

3 Observatorio Andalusi, *Estudio demográfico de la población musulmana: Explotación estadística del censo de ciudadanos musulmanes en España referido a fecha 31 de diciembre de 2018* (*Demographic Study of the Census of Muslim Citizens in Spain Conducted 31 December 2019*) (Madrid: Unión de Comunidades Islámicas de España, 2019), http://observatorio.hispanomuslim.es, accessed 19 February 2020.

Castilla-La Mancha (two) and Canarias (one). During the 2020–2021 school year, the department of education of the Catalan autonomous government developed a pilot plan in four primary schools in Catalonia.

The requirements that teachers of Islamic religious education must meet are regulated by Royal Decree 696/2007. Candidates must have the academic requirements demanded for other teachers (the diploma of *Magisterio*, a three-year university degree course in education for primary schools, or *Licenciatura* for secondary schools, or a five-year university degree of education) and have a declaration of eligibility or equivalent certification from the CIE.

Real Decreto 696/2007, de 1 de junio, por el que se regula la relación laboral de los profesores de religión prevista en la disposición adicional tercera de la Ley Orgánica 2/2006, de 3 de mayo, de Educación.
BOE núm. 138, de 9 de junio de 2007

Artículo 3. Requisitos exigibles.
1. Para impartir las enseñanzas de religión será necesario reunir los mismos requisitos de titulación exigibles, o equivalentes, en el respectivo nivel educativo, a los funcionarios docentes no universitarios conforme se enumeran en la Ley Orgánica 2/2006, de 3 de mayo, de Educación, haber sido propuestos por la Autoridad de la Confesión religiosa para impartir dicha enseñanza y haber obtenido la declaración de idoneidad o certificación equivalente de la confesión religiosa objeto de la materia educativa, todo ello con carácter previo a su contratación por la Administración competente.
2. Para ser contratado como profesor de religión, serán necesarios los siguientes requisitos:
a) Ser español o nacional de alguno de los Estados Miembros de la Unión Europea o nacional de algún Estado al que en virtud de los Tratados Internacionales celebrados por la Unión Europea y ratificados por España sea de aplicación la libre circulación de trabajadores, o ser extranjero con residencia legal en España y autorizado a trabajar o en disposición de obtener una autorización de trabajo por cuenta ajena.
b) Tener cumplidos 18 años de edad.
c) No padecer enfermedad ni estar afectado por limitación física o psíquica incompatible con el desempeño de las correspondientes funciones.
d) No haber sido separado, mediante expediente disciplinario, del servicio de cualquier Administración Pública, ni hallarse inhabilitado para el ejercicio de sus funciones. Los aspirantes cuya nacionalidad no sea la española deberán acreditar igualmente no estar sometidos a sanción dis-

ciplinaria o condena penal que impida en su Estado de origen el desempeño de sus funciones.

Ley Orgánica 2/2006, de 3 de mayo, de Educación.
BOE núm. 106, de 04 de mayo de 2006

Capítulo II Profesorado de las distintas enseñanzas

Artículo 92. Profesorado de educación infantil.
1. La atención educativa directa a los niños del primer ciclo de educación infantil correrá a cargo de profesionales que posean el título de Maestro con la especialización en educación infantil o el título de Grado equivalente y, en su caso, de otro personal con la debida titulación para la atención a las niñas y niños de esta edad [...]

Artículo 93. Profesorado de educación primaria.
1. Para impartir las enseñanzas de educación primaria será necesario tener el título de Maestro de educación primaria o el título de Grado equivalente, sin perjuicio de la habilitación de otras titulaciones universitarias que, a efectos de docencia pudiera establecer el Gobierno para determinadas áreas, previa consulta a las Comunidades Autónomas [...]
Artículo 94. Profesorado de educación secundaria obligatoria y de bachillerato.
Para impartir las enseñanzas de educación secundaria obligatoria y de bachillerato será necesario tener el título de Grado universitario o titulación equivalente, además de la formación pedagógica y didáctica de nivel de Postgrado, de acuerdo con lo dispuesto en el artículo 100 de la presente Ley, sin perjuicio de la habilitación de otras titulaciones que, a efectos de docencia pudiera establecer el Gobierno para determinadas áreas, previa consulta a las Comunidades Autónomas [...]

The teaching staff chosen by the CIE must also "speak fluent Spanish". The autonomous communities, in turn, can add further requirements, such as the command of any co-official languages.

Requisitos que debe reunir el profesorado de enseñanza islámica (Comisión Islámica de España)[4]

4 See https://comisionislamica.org/wp-content/uploads/2020/11/Requisitos-que-debe-reunir-el-profesorado-de-ensenanza-islamica.pdf, accessed 3 November 2020.

– Poseer titulación académica igual o equivalente a la exigida para la educación infantil o primaria o secundaria y bachillerato, al correspondiente profesorado además de la declaración de idoneidad de la Comisión Islámica de España.
– Tener cumplidos 18 años de edad y no haber alcanzado la edad de jubilación forzosa.
– Reunir los requisitos relativos a poseer nacionalidad española o comunitaria, u otra con residencia legal y autorización de trabajo.
– No haber sido separado mediante expediente disciplinario de cualquiera de las Administraciones Públicas ni hallarse inhabilitado para el desempeño de funciones públicas.
– No estar afectado por incompatibilidad o tener concedida la necesaria autorización de compatibilidad.
– No haber sido condenado por sentencia firme por algún delito contra la libertad e indemnidad sexual, que incluye la agresión y abuso sexual, exhibicionismo y provocación sexual, prostitución y explotación sexual y corrupción de menores, así como por trata de seres humanos.

The Cooperation Agreement recognised the right of Muslim communities to open Islamic schools in Spain. Today, the only two private Islamic schools in Madrid are associated with the Embassies of Libya (*Al Nahda Al Gadida* School) and Saudi Arabia (*Umm al-Qura School*) which belongs to the Madrid Islamic Cultural Centre complex.

Parallel to the development of this more formal Islamic religious education, the communities themselves started various religious socialisation initiatives, focused on children, youth and women, and based on a traditional model of religious transmission (*kuttab*, or Qur'anic schools). Muslim Qur'anic schools act as points to connect the communities with their societies and cultures of origin. Being connected to the background the students' origin represents means that religious socialisation in these informal contexts is carried out through a specific cultural heritage. Many of these initiatives are considered by parents to be complementary to the education their children receive in school, even though they are outside the structured, formalised school environment.

In 2006, UCIDE, with funding from the Foundation for Pluralism and Coexistence, published the first textbook on Islam, *Descubrir el Islam* (Discovering Islam), addressed to primary education. In 2009 the textbook for secondary education was published.[5]

5 From 2006 to 2017, the text manuals corresponding to the six primary levels were edited. Their publisher is Akal (see https://www.akal.com/libro/descubrir-el-islam-10_34464/, accessed 12 September 2014).

CHAPTER 8

Higher Education and Universities

In addition to what is established in article 10.6 of the Cooperation Agreement, the ability to establish Islamic universities and imam training centres is also guaranteed by Organic Law 4/2007 on Universities, which modifies the Organic Law on Universities of 2001. This Law provides that the Government shall regulate the civil effects of these studies.

Ley 26/1992, de 10 de noviembre, por la que se aprueba el Acuerdo de Cooperación del Estado con la Comisión Islámica de España

Artículo 10.6

La Comisión Islámica de España», así como las Comunidades pertenecientes a la misma, podrán establecer y dirigir […] Universidades y Centros de Formación Islámica, con sometimiento a la legislación general vigente en la materia

Ley Orgánica 4/2007, de 12 de abril, por la que se modifica la Ley Orgánica 6/2001, de 21 de diciembre, de Universidades.
«BOE» núm. 89, de 13 de abril de 2007

Disposición adicional undécima. Reconocimiento de efectos civiles:
El Gobierno, a propuesta de los ministerios competentes en materia de justicia y universidades, en aplicación de lo establecido en los Acuerdos de Cooperación entre el Estado y la Federación de Entidades Religiosas Evangélicas de España, aprobado por la Ley 24/1992, de 10 de noviembre, la Federación de Comunidades Israelitas de España, aprobado por la Ley 25/1992, de 10 de noviembre, y la Comisión Islámica de España, aprobado por la Ley 26/1992, de 10 de noviembre, regulará las condiciones para el reconocimiento de efectos civiles de los títulos académicos relativos a enseñanzas, de nivel universitario, de carácter teológico y de formación de ministros de culto, impartidas en centros docentes de nivel superior dependientes de las mencionadas entidades religiosas. […]

But, nowadays, apart from Catholic theology faculties, only the Protestant theology faculties of higher education have enjoyed the recognition of civil effects, after providing courses in theology for decades without official recognition.

The first Islamic higher education initiatives in Spain began shortly after the signing of the Cooperation Agreement in 1992. In 1995 the International Islamic University Averroes 'Ibn Rushd' of Al-Andalus was created in Córdoba, on the initiative of the Moroccan professor, Ali Kettani. This university offered Arabic language and Islamic science courses taught by Muslim teachers, but never obtained official recognition from the Spanish educational authorities. It had a very short history. It was closed because of the loss of institutional and financial support after the death of its director in 2001.

As the Muslim community in Spain developed, the need to train imams and community leaders became imperative. Currently, a significant number of imams come from Muslim countries with little knowledge of the social, political and legal reality of Spain. Some Muslim communities have organised several imam training seminars, informally and on weekends, but none of them has received official recognition so far. Large Muslim centres, such as the Fuengirola mosque and the two largest mosques in Madrid (Abu Bakr in the Estrecho neighbourhood, and the Islamic Cultural Centre of Madrid-Omar ibn-Jattab mosque) have periodically organised training activities in which imams from all over Spain have taken part.

Following the signing of the 1992 Cooperation Agreement, the Islamic Commission of Spain initiated an internal consultation to propose a training programme for imams. These projects were never completed due to internal disagreements. Therefore, each federation offered its own training initiatives for its imams. The new board of directors of the CIE has proposed the creation of a commission of imams and training, which to date has not published any concrete proposal.

So far, the most significant initiatives have been proposed from outside the two main Islamic federations. The first initiatives to be highlighted were proposed by a public university, the National University of Distance Learning (UNED), and a private one, the University Camilo José Cela. This latter university centre organised a course under the title of "Islamic religion and culture". This training was with the collaboration of the Islamic Board, the entity founded by Mansur Escudero, secretary general of the FEERI, and was given between the years 2005 and 2011. The National University of Distance Learning (UNED) organised, alongside the *Pluralism and Coexistence Foundation*, a course called "Islam and Democratic Principles" taught in the period 2009–2011, after which it disappeared. The characteristic of both training initiatives is that they were based on distance training. The fact that they did not include theological content but varied aspects on Islamic culture and on the Spanish legal framework on religious freedom did not favour either the participation in the study of Islam of active imams or the enrolment of interested non-Muslim students. Diplomas obtained by students at both university centres were not official. They were private documents recognised by those universities alone.

Apart from these two initiatives with the participation of university centres, there were others organised by different Muslim federations at the regional level. These are courses organised by the Islamic and Cultural Council of Catalonia, a federation of Muslim entities based in Catalonia, and the Islamic Federation of Murcia. In Catalonia since 2003 a collaboration agreement has been established with the regional government to initiate training in language and the social and institutional context of this society, aimed at the imams of the communities that were federated in this entity. From 2006 to 2010 this training included theological content, in collaboration with the Ministry of Religious Affairs of Morocco, with the support of the Department of Religious Affairs of the Generalitat of Catalonia. After passing this training, imams obtained a diploma that had no official recognition.

When the Islamic Federation of Murcia proposed its course in 2007, it was not yet part of the Islamic Commission of Spain (CIE). Its main leader, Mounir Benjelloun, would later become the secretary general of FEERI. Initially, the aim of this training was not only to offer theological training but to provide basic education on Islam. The teachers who participated for the first time in this course came mainly from Belgium, France, Spain, Morocco and Egypt, and were offered subjects such as *fiqh* or *tafsir*, but also Spanish, computer and internet classes, and public speaking skills. As a continuation of these courses, in 2013 FEERI proposed training which was expanded in content and duration (two years), and which was specifically aimed at imams. This training would take place at weekends at the headquarters of the *Assalam Mosque* in Valencia. This course was organised together with the *Muslim Federation of the Valencian Community* (FEMCOVA), the *Spanish League of Imams* and in cooperation with the European Institute of Islamic Sciences and the Islamic University of Rotterdam.

In September 2016, the project to create the first Islamic University of Spain, which would be in San Sebastián (Basque Country), was announced. The initiative, linked to the Islamic University of Minnesota (USA), should have started its virtual classes in the 2016–2017 academic year, but the classes have not begun, with no reasons given for this delay. Its head, Rachid Boutarbouch, is related to the Moroccan movement, Justice and Charity. The university's headquarters have since 2019 moved to Barcelona, to the headquarters of the Islamic Centre entitled "House of science and knowledge".[1] This university has

1 See its website under construction https://www.universityiius.org/.

been registered in the Murcia Commercial Register since April 2018 in the name of the current FEERI Secretary General, Mounir Benjelloun. For the 2020–2021 academic year, the university is offerings a four-year degree in Islamic studies of 240 ECTS, in Spanish and online.

The most recent training initiative aimed at Muslim imams and religious leaders is the diploma from the University of Zaragoza entitled "Religion and Law in a democratic society: challenges of coexistence in a plural context". This course has been organized jointly with the Islamic Commission of Spain since 2018 and includes a total of 45 ECTS, but it does not include subjects of Islamic theology.

CHAPTER 9

Islamic Chaplaincy in Public Institutions

The 1992 Cooperation Agreement between the State and the CIE recognises in article 8 that Muslim military personnel serving in the Armed Forces have the right to receive Islamic spiritual guidance.

Ley 26/1992, de 10 de noviembre, por la que se aprueba el Acuerdo de Cooperación del Estado con la Comisión Islámica de España

Artículo 8:

1. Se reconoce el derecho de los militares españoles musulmanes, sean o no profesionales, y de cuantas personas de dicha religión presten servicio en las Fuerzas Armadas, a recibir asistencia religiosa islámica y a participar en actividades y ritos religiosos propios del islam, previa la oportuna autorización de sus jefes, que procurarán hacer compatibles con las necesidades del servicio, facilitando los lugares y medios adecuados para su desarrollo.
2. Los militares musulmanes que no puedan cumplir sus obligaciones religiosas islámicas, especialmente la oración colectiva en común del viernes, por no haber mezquita o, en su caso, oratorio en el lugar de su destino, podrán ser autorizados para el cumplimiento de aquéllas en la mezquita u oratorio de la localidad más próxima, cuando las necesidades del servicio lo permitan.
3. La asistencia religiosa islámica será dispensada por los Imanes o personas designadas con carácter estable por las Comunidades Islámicas pertenecientes a la «Comisión Islámica de España», autorizados por los mandos correspondientes que prestarán la colaboración precisa para el desempeño de sus funciones en términos de igualdad con los ministros de culto de otras Iglesias, Confesiones o Comunidades religiosas que tengan firmados Acuerdos de Cooperación con el Estado.
4. Las autoridades correspondientes comunicarán el fallecimiento de los militares musulmanes, ocurrido durante la prestación del servicio, a la familia del fallecido.

But this right has not yet been implemented. In its annual report, the *Observatorio Andalusi*[1] denounces the situation of discrimination that occurs with respect to Islamic religious assistance in the Spanish armed forces. When the Military Career Law was published in 2007 (Law 39/2007, of November 19), the right of soldiers to receive religious assistance was recognised, but in practice it is limited to Catholic soldiers through the Military Archbishopric.

Ley 39/2007, de 19 de noviembre, de la carrera militar.
«BOE» núm. 278, de 20 de noviembre de 2007

Disposición adicional octava. Servicio de Asistencia Religiosa.
1. El Gobierno garantizará la asistencia religiosa a los miembros de las Fuerzas Armadas en los términos previstos en el ordenamiento.
2. La asistencia religioso-pastoral a los miembros católicos de las Fuerzas Armadas se ejerce por medio del Arzobispado Castrense, en los términos del Acuerdo de 3 de enero de 1979 entre el Estado español y la Santa Sede, prestándose por los Cuerpos Eclesiásticos del Ejército de Tierra, de la Armada y del Ejército del Aire, declarados a extinguir, y por el Servicio de Asistencia Religiosa de las Fuerzas Armadas.
Los sacerdotes integrados en el Servicio de Asistencia Religiosa, que son capellanes castrenses en los términos que establece el citado acuerdo con la Santa Sede, se regirán por lo previsto en él, por la legislación canónica correspondiente y por esta disposición.
Para la atención religioso-pastoral se podrán establecer convenios con diócesis y órdenes religiosas para incorporar, a propuesta del Arzobispo Castrense, sacerdotes colaboradores.
3. Los militares evangélicos, judíos o musulmanes podrán recibir asistencia religiosa de su propia confesión, si lo desean, de conformidad con lo determinado en los correspondientes acuerdos de cooperación establecidos entre el Estado español y la Federación de Entidades Religiosas Evangélicas de España, Federación de Comunidades Israelitas de España y Comisión Islámica de España.
4. Los demás militares profesionales podrán recibir, si lo desean, asistencia religiosa de ministros de culto de las iglesias, confesiones o comuni-

1 Observatorio Andalusi, *Estudio demográfico de la población musulmana: Explotación estadística del censo de ciudadanos musulmanes en España referido a fecha 31 de diciembre de 2018* (*Demographic Study of the Census of Muslim Citizens in Spain Conducted 31 December 2019*) (Madrid: Unión de Comunidades Islámicas de España, 2019), http://observatorio.hispanomuslim.es, accessed 19 February 2020.

dades religiosas, inscritas en el Registro de Entidades Religiosas, en los términos previstos en el ordenamiento y en su caso, de conformidad con lo que se establezca en los correspondientes acuerdos de cooperación entre el Estado español y dichas entidades. [...]

Hitherto, no military imam has been recognised even though, as indicated in the report by the *Observatorio Andalusi*, there are army units (as is the case of the Regulars, established in Ceuta and Melilla) which have Muslim soldiers.

Article 9 of CA also recognises that hospital and prison inmates are entitled to receive spiritual guidance from imams or persons duly appointed by the Islamic communities, subject to the authorisation of the Islamic Community of Spain.

Ley 26/1992, de 10 de noviembre, por la que se aprueba el Acuerdo de Cooperación del Estado con la Comisión Islámica de España

Artículo 9:
1. Se garantiza el ejercicio del derecho a la asistencia religiosa de los internados en centros o establecimientos penitenciarios, hospitalarios, asistenciales u otros análogos del sector público, proporcionada por los Imanes o personas designadas por las Comunidades, que deberán ser autorizados por los organismos administrativos competentes. Las direcciones de los centros o establecimientos públicos estarán obligadas a transmitir a la Comunidad Islámica correspondiente las solicitudes de asistencia religiosa recibidas de los internos o de sus familiares, si los propios interesados no estuvieran en condiciones de hacerlo. La asistencia religiosa prevista en este artículo comprenderá la que se dispense a los moribundos, así como las honras fúnebres del rito islámico.
2. En todo caso, la asistencia religiosa a que se refiere el número anterior se prestará con pleno respeto al principio de libertad religiosa y con observancia de las normas de organización y régimen interno de los centros, libre y sin limitación de horario. Por lo que se refiere a los establecimientos penitenciarios, la asistencia religiosa se realizará de acuerdo con lo dispuesto en la legislación penitenciaria.
3. Los gastos que origine el desarrollo de la asistencia religiosa serán sufragados en la forma que acuerden los representantes de la «Comisión Islámica de España», con la dirección de los centros y establecimientos públicos contemplados en el número 1 de este artículo, sin perjuicio de la utilización de los locales que, a tal fin, existan en dichos centros o establecimientos.

But in this case the regulation on prison inmates has been implemented for denominations that, like Islam, have signed a cooperation agreement with the State through Royal Decree 710/2006.[2] Regarding the requirements for authorisation, this decree establishes that the religious assistant is obliged to present a certificate of not having a criminal record, to have legal residence (if they are foreigners, they do not need a work permit if they dedicate purely to religious activities) and to follow "courses or training sessions" in penitentiary matters if the prison organises them and establishes that they are mandatory. In any case, once the application issued by the denomination proposing a religious assistant has been submitted, the administration must deal with it within four months; if not, it shall be understood as granted by what is known as "positive administrative silence". The authorisation to develop Islamic chaplaincy is valid for a year and can be renewed annually, except in the case of a reasoned decision against it. The authorisation can be cancelled at the end of the year (or at any time) in one of three ways: cessation, revocation or suspension.

Real Decreto 710/2006, de 9 de junio, de desarrollo de los Acuerdos de Cooperación firmados por el Estado con la Federación de Entidades Religiosas Evangélicas de España, la Federación de Comunidades Judías de España y la Comisión Islámica de España, en el ámbito de la asistencia religiosa penitenciaria.
BOE núm. 138, de 10 de junio de 2006

Artículo 7. Cese, revocación y suspensión de la autorización:
1. Los ministros de culto acreditados cesarán en sus actividades a iniciativa propia o de la autoridad religiosa de la que dependan, debiendo comunicarse dicha decisión a la Administración penitenciaria competente.
2. La autorización podrá ser revocada por la Administración penitenciaria que la concedió cuando el ministro de culto realice actividades no previstas en el régimen de la asistencia religiosa, fueren contrarias al régimen del centro o a la normativa penitenciaria, previa audiencia del interesado y mediante resolución motivada.
3. También procederá la revocación cuando se produzca un incumplimiento sobrevenido de los requisitos que justificaron su otorgamiento.

2 Royal Decree 710/2006, of 9 June, developing the Cooperation Agreements signed by the State with the Federation of Evangelical Religious Entities of Spain, the Federation of Jewish Communities of Spain and the Islamic Commission of Spain, in the field of prison religious assistance.

4. Si la actividad del ministro de culto atentara gravemente contra el régimen y seguridad del centro, o conculcara el ordenamiento jurídico, el director del centro podrá suspender cautelarmente la autorización, mediante resolución motivada, hasta tanto no se pronuncie el órgano competente sobre la revocación.

This norm also establishes that the financing of material expenses and personnel will be done in accordance with the provisions of the Cooperation Agreements with the State.

Artículo 11. Régimen económico. La financiación de los gastos materiales y de personal que ocasione la asistencia religiosa se realizará de conformidad con lo dispuesto en los Acuerdos de Cooperación con el Estado y en la legislación aplicable en cada caso.

As Cooperation Agreements between the State and federations of Jews (article 9.3) and Protestants (article 9.4) establish that the costs of religious assistance "will be covered by the respective communities", their respective religious communities (Jews and Protestants) must pay the salaries of chaplains.

Nevertheless, the Cooperation Agreement with CIE establishes in its article 9.3 that these costs will be covered in the form agreed by CIE and public authorities.

Ley 26/1992, de 10 de noviembre, por la que se aprueba el Acuerdo de Cooperación del Estado con la Comisión Islámica de España
Artículo 9.3. Los gastos que origine el desarrollo de la asistencia religiosa serán sufragados en la forma que acuerden los representantes de la «Comisión Islámica de España», con la dirección de los centros y establecimientos públicos contemplados en el número 1 de este artículo, sin perjuicio de la utilización de los locales que, a tal fin, existan en dichos centros o establecimientos.

Following this article, on 24 October 2007 the CIE and the State signed a collaboration agreement for the public funding of religious assistance for Muslim inmates in prisons. This agreement establishes that the Ministry of the Interior will pay the salaries of Muslim chaplains if they have at least ten inmates in the same penitentiary.

Convenio de colaboración del estado con la comisión islámica de España para la financiación de los gastos que ocasione el desarrollo de la asis-

tencia religiosa en los establecimientos penitenciarios de competencia estatal.
Madrid a 24 de Octubre de 2007

Anexo I: La cuantía que deberá ser abonada a cada asistente religioso dependerá de la demanda de asistencia religiosa efectivamente acreditada, de acuerdo con el siguiente baremo: hasta 50 internos se les considera a media jornada, de 51 a 150 se les considera jornada complete y si excede de 150 internos se considerará una jornada completa y media jornada. La jornada completa tendrá una duración de seis horas y tres horas la media jornada.

So the salaries of Muslim chaplains can be paid by the State, while Jews and Evangelical chaplains must be paid, in compliance with their Agreements of Cooperation, by their respective Jewish or Protestant communities.

Requisitos que debe reunir el candidato a asistente religioso (Comisión Islámica de España)[3]
- Certificado negativo de antecedentes penales en España del Ministerio de Justicia, y en el caso de ser extranjero también en el país de origen.
- Certificado de una Comunidad religiosa, de pertenencia, designación y dedicación con carácter estable al ministerio religioso, a conformar y designar por la CIE.
- Afiliación a la Seguridad Social.
- Indicación del centro o centros ante los que se solicita acreditación.

In March 2015, the Ministry of the Interior signed a collaboration agreement with the Islamic Commission of Spain to guarantee religious care in the detention centres for foreigners (CIE: Centros de Internamiento de Extranjeros). It is an agreement that is renewed annually and does not involve any public funding.[4]

There are 84 prisons in Spain. Seventy-two of them depend on the Ministry of the Interior, and another 12 on the regional government of Catalonia,

3 See https://comisionislamica.org/wp-content/uploads/2021/01/Requisitos-que-debe-reunir-el-candidato-a-asistente-religioso.pdf, accessed 3 November 2020.

4 See the text of the agreement at https://transparencia.gob.es/servicios-buscador/contenido/conveniosyencomiendas.htm?id=Convenio_INT201500491&lang=es&fcAct=2019-12-09T11:17:09.579Z, accessed 10 November 2019.

which has taken over the competences in terms of prison services.[5] According to the *Observatorio Andalusi*, 20 imams offer chaplaincy services in prisons, and another seven in Spanish hospitals. There are no imams providing chaplaincy services in the armed forces.

Spanish prisons have reoriented religious assistance to make it a mechanism for preventing the radicalisation of inmates. Prison authorities look at the reports by the Spanish National Intelligence Centre to determine the adequacy of these imams. Since 2019 the Interior Ministry has developed a monitoring programme for prisoners convicted of jihadism, which includes different measures to prevent them from influencing the radicalisation of other prisoners.

5 See http://justicia.gencat.cat/web/.content/home/departament/convenis_i_acords/2019/conv-fed-consell-islamic.pdf, accessed 25 July 2019.

CHAPTER 10

Employment, Festivals and Social Law

According to the Religious Freedom Act (LOLR), one manifestation of religious freedom is the right to celebrate religious feasts, which includes the right to observe days of rest and to celebrate holidays and ceremonies in accordance with the precepts of one's religion or belief.[1]

This manifestation of religious freedom depends on the current labour legislation. Spanish labour legislation recognises weekly holidays and festivals throughout the year. Regarding weekly days of rest, the general Labour Act (Workers' Statute)[2] establishes that employees are entitled to rest for one and a half days a week, usually Sunday and either Saturday afternoon or Monday morning.

Real Decreto Legislativo 2/2015, de 23 de octubre, por el que se aprueba el texto refundido de la Ley del Estatuto de los Trabajadores
BOE núm. 255 de 24 de octubre de 2015

Artículo 37.1:
Los trabajadores tendrán derecho a un descanso mínimo semanal, acumulable por periodos de hasta catorce días, de día y medio ininterrumpido que, como regla general, comprenderá la tarde del sábado o, en su caso, la mañana del lunes y el día completo del domingo

The Cooperation Agreement between the Spanish State and the Holy See concerning legal affairs also states that "the State recognises Sunday as a holiday".

Instrumento de Ratificación del Acuerdo entre el Estado español y la Santa Sede sobre asuntos jurídicos, firmado el 3 de enero de 1979 en la Ciudad del Vaticano.

Artículo III: El Estado reconoce como días festivos todos los domingos. De común acuerdo se determinará qué otras festividades religiosas son reconocidas como días festivos.

1 Art. 6.1. h of the Declaration 36/55 of 25 November 1981 on the elimination of all forms of intolerance and of discrimination based on religion or belief (General Assembly United Nations).

2 Royal Legislative Decree 2/2015, of October 23, approving the revised text of the Law of the Workers' Statute.

But, according to the Spanish Constitutional Court, Sunday as the weekly day of rest is a secular institution without religious meaning, so the coincidence with Catholic festivity is based not on religious grounds but on tradition.[3] Article 12 of the AC with the Islamic Commission of Spain does not mention the weekly days of rest, unlike the Cooperation Agreement with the Jews.

Ley 26/1992, de 10 de noviembre, por la que se aprueba el Acuerdo de Cooperación del Estado con la Comisión Islámica de España

Artículo 12.1: Los miembros de las Comunidades Islámicas pertenecientes a la «Comisión Islámica de España» que lo deseen, podrán solicitar la interrupción de su trabajo los viernes de cada semana, día de rezo colectivo obligatorio y solemne de los musulmanes, desde las trece treinta hasta las dieciséis treinta horas, así como la conclusión de la jornada laboral una hora antes de la puesta del sol, durante el mes de ayuno (Ramadán). En ambos casos, será necesario el previo acuerdo entre las partes. Las horas dejadas de trabajar deberán ser recuperadas sin compensación alguna.

Ley 25/1992, de 10 de noviembre, por la que se aprueba el Acuerdo de Cooperación del Estado con la Federación de Comunidades Israelitas de España,

Artículo 12.1: El descanso laboral semanal, para los fieles de Comunidades Israelitas pertenecientes a la FCI, podrá comprender, siempre que medie acuerdo entre las partes, la tarde del viernes y el día completo del sábado, en sustitución del que establece el artículo 37.1 del Estatuto de los Trabajadores como regla general.

The AC mentions only that Muslim workers or employees are entitled to stop working in their place of work on Fridays from 1.30 to 4.30 p.m. to attend weekly mandatory congregational prayer, and to leave work an hour before sunset during the month of fasting (Ramadan), but only if there is a previous agreement between the employer and the employee (normally expressed within the contract). In that case, Muslim employees will be required to make up for the hours not worked with no compensation whatsoever. In those terms, the employer can avoid even considering the Muslim employee's request or deny it without

3 STC 19/1985, of 13 February.

offering any argument. It is the employer's decision. If the effectiveness of a fundamental right depends on the will of other person we are not really talking about religious freedom as a human right. It would be more in keeping with religious freedom if the general rule were that Muslims had the right to be entitled to those two manifestations of religious freedom described in the Agreement, unless it was not possible according to the specific nature of the job or the organisation. But so far, this is not what current law says.

Regarding other civil festivities throughout the year, article 37.2 of the Workers' Statute establishes that there cannot be more than 14, and two of them can be local festivals, but in any case, religious festivities as Christmas and New Year (and some others) are nationwide holidays.

> Estatuto de los Trabajadores
>
> Artículo 37.2: Las fiestas laborales, que tendrán carácter retribuido y no recuperable, no podrán exceder de catorce al año, de las cuales dos serán locales. En cualquier caso, se respetarán como fiestas de ámbito nacional las de la Natividad del Señor, Año Nuevo, 1 de mayo, como Fiesta del Trabajo, y 12 de octubre, como Fiesta Nacional de España.

Article 12 of the Cooperation agreement between the Spanish State and the Islamic Commission of Spain recognises some Islamic holidays that, at the request of Muslim employees, may replace the general holidays established in article 37.2 of the Workers' Statute, provided an agreement to this end is reached between employer and employee, as paid holidays that cannot be substituted for. The religious festivals which can be considered are Al Hijra; the Islamic New Year; the first day of the month of Muharram; Ashura, 10 Muharram; Mawlid al-Nabi, 12 Rabi al-Awwal, marking the celebration of the Prophet's birth; Laylat Al-Isra wa Al-Miraj, 27 Rajab, the night journey and Ascension of the Prophet; Eid Al-Fitr, 1, 2 and 3 Shawwal, marking the end of Ramadan; and Eid Al-Adha, 10, 11 and 12 Dhul-Hijjah, marking the anniversary of Abraham's sacrifice.

> Ley 26/1992, de 10 de noviembre, por la que se aprueba el Acuerdo de Cooperación del Estado con la Comisión Islámica de España
>
> Artículo 12.2; Las festividades y conmemoraciones que a continuación se expresan, que según la Ley Islámica tienen el carácter de religiosas, podrán sustituir, siempre que medie acuerdo entre las partes, a las establecidas con carácter general por el Estatuto de los Trabajadores, en su

artículo 37.2, con el mismo carácter de retribuidas y no recuperables, a petición de los fieles de las Comunidades Islámicas pertenecientes a la «Comisión Islámica de España»: AL HIYRA, correspondiente al 1.º de Muharram, primer día del Año Nuevo Islámico; ACHURA, décimo día de Muharram; IDU AL-MAULID, corresponde al 12 de Rabiu al Awwal, nacimiento del Profeta; AL ISRA WA AL-MIRAY, corresponde al 27 de Rayab, fecha del Viaje Nocturno y la Ascensión del Profeta; IDU AL-FITR, corresponde a los días 1.º, 2.º y 3.º de Shawwal y celebra la culminación del Ayuno de Ramadán; IDU AL-ADHA, corresponde a los días 10.º, 11.º y 12.º de Du Al-Hyyah y celebra el sacrificio protagonizado por el Profeta Abraham.

Muslim pupils studying in public schools or State-subsidised private schools shall be excused from attending class and taking exams on Fridays between 1.30 and 4.30 p.m. and on the holy days and religious festivals, at their own request or at the request of a parent or guardian. This decision relies only on them, not on the teachers. The Cooperation Agreements also establish that exams, competitive exams and civil service tests scheduled to take place on Fridays or on Muslim holy days and festivals may be held on alternative dates for Muslims who so request, provided there is no reason to prevent this.

Artículo 12.3: "Los alumnos musulmanes que cursen estudios en centros de enseñanza públicos o privados concertados, estarán dispensados de la asistencia a clase y de la celebración de exámenes, en el día del viernes durante las horas a que se refiere el número 1 de este artículo y en las festividades y conmemoraciones religiosas anteriormente expresadas, a petición propia o de quienes ejerzan la patria potestad o tutela".

Artículo 12.4: "Los exámenes, oposiciones o pruebas selectivas convocadas para el ingreso en las Administraciones Públicas, que hayan de celebrarse en los días a que se refiere el número anterior, serán señalados, para los musulmanes que lo soliciten, en una fecha alternativa, cuando no haya causa motivada que lo impida".

CHAPTER 11

Islamic Slaughter and Food Regulation

11.1 Food Regulations

The Cooperation Agreement between the Spanish State and the Islamic Commission of Spain allows the latter to request and obtain the trademark of "halal" denomination from the Patent and Trademark Office, so that they can control the correct use of the halal denomination in the market, both internal and export (article 14.1). But so far CIE has not done this. Nevertheless, an Islamic group, *Junta Islamica*, has done so. The "Halal Brand" was registered in 2013 in the Spanish Patent and Trademark Registry, with the support of the main certification company in Spain, the Halal Institute,[1] to regulate and certify food suitable for the consumption of Spanish Muslims and to be able to export these products from Spain to Islamic countries.

The 1992 agreement also includes a paragraph recognising that Muslim individuals in State centres and military barracks and Muslim pupils in public schools and State-subsidised private schools are entitled to request halal food and adapt mealtimes during the month of Ramadan.[2] The authorities have an obligation only to try to grant this right but not to grant it unconditionally.

Once these requirements have been fulfilled, these products must bear the mark of the Islamic Commission of Spain on their packaging as a guarantee that they have been prepared in accordance with Islamic dietary laws, for the purpose of their sale, import and export.

Ley 26/1992, de 10 de noviembre, por la que se aprueba el Acuerdo de Cooperación del Estado con la Comisión Islámica de España

Artículo 14
1. De acuerdo con la dimensión espiritual y las particularidades específicas de la Ley Islámica, la denominación «Halal» sirve para distinguir los productos alimentarios elaborados de acuerdo con la misma.
2. Para la protección del uso correcto de estas denominaciones, la «Comisión Islámica de España» deberá solicitar y obtener del Registro de la

1 See https://www.institutohalal.com/, accessed 10 November 2020.
2 AC article 12.1.

Propiedad Industrial los registros de marca correspondientes, de acuerdo con la normativa legal vigente. Cumplidos los requisitos anteriores, estos productos, a efectos de comercialización, importación y exportación, tendrán la garantía de haber sido elaborados con arreglo a la Ley Islámica, cuando lleven en sus envases el correspondiente distintivo de la «Comisión Islámica de España». [...]
4. La alimentación de los internados en centros o establecimientos públicos y dependencias militares, y la de los alumnos musulmanes de los centros docentes públicos y privados concertados que lo soliciten, se procurará adecuar a los preceptos religiosos islámicos, así como el horario de comidas durante el mes de ayuno (Ramadán).

11.2 Islamic Meals in Public Institutions

According to the Cooperation Agreement of 1992, the State must ensure that a halal menu is provided in public institutions such as hospitals, prisons and the army. In reality, these provisions of the law are not always followed. Muslim representatives have asked to have halal menus in schools and in hospitals and found different responses from those responsible for these centres.

11.3 Islamic Slaughter

The Cooperation Agreement between the Spanish State and the Islamic Commission of Spain establishes in article 14.3 that "the slaughter of animals in accordance with Islamic law must meet prevailing health standards".

Ley 26/1992, de 10 de noviembre, por la que se aprueba el Acuerdo de Cooperación del Estado con la Islámica de España Comisión

Artículo 14.3. El sacrificio de animales que se realice de acuerdo con las Leyes Islámicas deberá respetar la normativa sanitaria vigente.

In Spain the legislation on animal welfare requires that animals must be stunned before they are slaughtered. But this rule has exceptions prescribed by religious ritual, in particular Jewish and Muslim traditions. Law 32/2007 of 7 November 2007 on the care, transport, experimentation on and slaughter of animals allows for their slaughter in accordance with religious rites and without previous stunning if such rites do not breach one of the limitations on religious freedom, e.g. public order, which includes public health, public moral and public security grounds. And ritual slaughter must be performed under the supervision, and according to, the instructions of the public veterinary surgeon.

Article 6.3 3 of the Law determines that if the sacrifice of animals following the rites of churches, confessions or religious communities registered in the Registry of Religious Entities and the obligations in terms of stunning are incompatible with the prescriptions of the respective religious rite, the authorities will not demand compliance with these obligations as long as the practices do not exceed the limits referred to in article 3 of Organic Law 7/1980, of 5 July, on Religious Freedom (public order). In any case, sacrifice according to the religious rite in question will be made under the supervision and in accordance with the instructions of the official veterinary surgeon. The slaughterhouse must notify the competent authority of the performance of this type of slaughter to be registered for that purpose, without prejudice to the authorisation provided for in European Union regulations.

Ley 32/2007, de 7 de noviembre, para el cuidado de los animales, en su explotación, transporte, experimentación y sacrificio
BOE núm. 268, de 08/11/2007

Artículo 6. Sacrificio o matanza de animales.
1. Las normas sobre la construcción, las instalaciones y los equipos de los mataderos, así como su funcionamiento, evitarán a los animales agitación, dolor o sufrimiento innecesarios.
2. El sacrificio de animales fuera de los mataderos se hará únicamente en los supuestos previstos por la normativa aplicable en cada caso y de acuerdo con los requisitos fijados por ésta, a excepción de los sacrificios de animales llevados a cabo por veterinarios con fines diagnósticos.
3. Cuando el sacrificio de los animales se realice según los ritos propios de Iglesias, Confesiones o Comunidades religiosas inscritas en el Registro de Entidades Religiosas, y las obligaciones en materia de aturdimiento sean incompatibles con las prescripciones del respectivo rito religioso, las autoridades competentes no exigirán el cumplimiento de dichas obligaciones siempre que las prácticas no sobrepasen los límites a los que se refiere el artículo 3 de la Ley Orgánica 7/1980, de 5 de julio, de Libertad Religiosa.
En todo caso, el sacrificio conforme al rito religioso de que se trate se realizará bajo la supervisión y de acuerdo con las instrucciones del veterinario oficial.

El matadero deberá comunicar a la autoridad competente que se va a realizar este tipo de sacrificios para ser registrado al efecto, sin perjuicio de la autorización prevista en la normativa comunitaria.

In this sense, the main problem that arises has to do with the sacrifice that is made during the feast of Eid al-Adha, since a significant number of Muslim families celebrate this feast by sacrificing a lamb themselves. This supposes a whole set of health risks, regarding which health administrations have had to take measures. In the case of the cities of Ceuta and Melilla, given the relevance of this holiday, the local authorities have had to set up spaces and mechanisms for collecting the waste generated by the sacrifice. In the case of Catalonia, in 2015 the regional government drew up a set of recommendations aimed at Muslim communities so that they were aware of the illegality of a sacrifice outside a controlled health context, and that they delegated the sacrifice to meat traders they trusted.[3]

3 See *La fiesta del sacrificio en Cataluña. Descripción y normativa sanitaria* (The feast of sacrifice in Catalonia. Description and sanitary regulations), http://justicia.gencat.cat/ca/ambits/afers-religiosos/publicacions/sacrifici/, accessed 10 November 2020.

CHAPTER 12

Family Law

12.1 Islamic Marriage

The civil Code allows marriage to be celebrated according to either civil or religious celebration (article 49), but only those religious forms established by denominations that have signed a cooperation agreement with the State or that have deeply rooted character can be used (article 60).

Código Civil español
Real Decreto de 24 de julio de 1889 por el que se publica el Código Civil

Artículo 49: "Cualquier español podrá contraer matrimonio dentro o fuera de España:
1.º En la forma regulada en este Código.
2.º En la forma religiosa legalmente prevista. También podrá contraer matrimonio fuera de España con arreglo a la forma establecida por la ley del lugar de celebración".

Artículo 60:
1. El matrimonio celebrado según las normas del Derecho canónico o en cualquiera de otras formas religiosas previstas en los acuerdos de cooperación entre el Estado y las confesiones religiosas produce efectos civiles.
2. Igualmente, se reconocen efectos civiles al matrimonio celebrado en la forma religiosa prevista por las iglesias, confesiones, comunidades religiosas o federaciones de las mismas que, inscritas en el Registro de Entidades Religiosas, hayan obtenido el reconocimiento de notorio arraigo en España. En este supuesto, el reconocimiento de efectos civiles requerirá el cumplimiento de los siguientes requisitos: a) La tramitación de un acta o expediente previo de capacidad matrimonial con arreglo a la normativa del Registro Civil. b) La libre manifestación del consentimiento ante un ministro de culto debidamente acreditado y dos testigos mayores de edad. La condición de ministro de culto será acreditada mediante certificación expedida por la iglesia, confesión o comunidad religiosa que haya obtenido el reconocimiento de notorio arraigo en España, con la conformidad de la federación que, en su caso, hubiere solicitado dicho reconocimiento.

The Spanish State allows not only civil but also some religious marriages. But the State only grants civil effects to the form of celebration, not to the rest of the religious regulation on marriage (mutual rights and duties, dissolution, nullity, etc.). However, regarding to Catholic marriage the legal system recognises not only Catholic religious celebration but also the civil effects of marriage annulment and pontifical decision of dissolution of valid but non-consummated marriage.[1]

As is established in the cooperation agreement signed between Islam and the State, Islamic marriage celebration has civil effects. If two people wish to have an Islamic marriage in Spain, they must take the following steps. First, they must prove before the competent officials of the Civil Registry that they fulfil the legal requirements for getting married in accordance with articles 46–47 of the Civil Code.

Código Civil español

Artículo 46: No pueden contraer matrimonio:
1. Los menores de edad no emancipados.
2. Los que estén ligados con vínculo matrimonial.

Artículo 47: Tampoco pueden contraer matrimonio entre sí:
1. Los parientes en línea recta por consanguinidad o adopción.
2. Los colaterales por consanguinidad hasta el tercer grado.
3. Los condenados por haber tenido participación en la muerte dolosa del cónyuge o persona con la que hubiera estado unida por análoga relación de afectividad a la conyugal.

Although the Cooperation Agreement with CIE does not require this checking prior to the marriage celebration (it can be fulfilled afterwards), it is highly recommended by the State.[2] If the bride and groom choose do the checking before the Civil Registry prior to marriage, as is recommended but not compulsory, once this check has been completed, the competent official of the Civil Registry (court clerk, notary, the corresponding official or Judge of the

1 In contrast with the other denominations that have signed a Cooperation Agreement in 1992, with respect to canonical marriage law, the Agreement on Legal Affairs signed by the Spanish State and the Holy See in 1979 recognises civil effectiveness not only to the form of canonical celebration but also to declarations of nullity and pontifical decisions regarding a marriage that is non-consummated, "at the request of the parties" and provided that the competent civil court declares them "in accordance with the law of the State" (Article VI.1 & 2).

2 Instruction of the General Direction of Registries and Notaries on 10 February 1993.

Civil Registry Office or the diplomatic officer or consular agent in charge of the consulate's Civil Register) must issue the parties with a certificate in duplicate stating that they are legally entitled to contract marriage—a 'certificate of marital capacity'.

As this certificate is valid for six months, the religious ceremony must be celebrated within that period before an imam or Islamic leader and two witnesses of legal age (over 18 years old). Once the marriage is celebrated, the imam or Islamic leader enters in both copies the date of the celebration, the names of the imam and witnesses and a certification that the witnesses are of legal age. This certificate must include the particulars required by the Civil Registry laws.

One of the copies remains in the archives of the Islamic community in which the marriage was held, as a record of its celebration. The representative of the Islamic Community will send the other copy to the Civil Registry, certifying that the marriage has taken place, so that it is duly registered. Although the marriage has legal effects from the moment of celebration, its full recognition will not take place until its registration in the Civil Registry (article 7.1 of the Cooperation Agreement with CIE and article 61 of the Civil Code).

If the procedure for checking the matrimonial capacity has not been accomplished before the religious wedding, as is recommended, the checking should be done by the competent official of the Civil Registry after the Islamic celebration and before registration. In this case, the check affects not only the formal requirements for the celebration but also the substantive requirements (articles 44–48). Only then will the judge or official proceed to register the marriage in the Civil Registry.

Código Civil español

Artículo 44: El hombre y la mujer tienen derecho a contraer matrimonio conforme a las disposiciones de este Código. El matrimonio tendrá los mismos requisitos y efectos cuando ambos contrayentes sean del mismo o de diferente sexo.

Artículo 45: No hay matrimonio sin consentimiento matrimonial. La condición, término o modo del consentimiento se tendrá por no puesto.

Artículo 46: No pueden contraer matrimonio: 1. Los menores de edad no emancipados. 2. Los que estén ligados con vínculo matrimonial.
Artículo 47: Tampoco pueden contraer matrimonio entre sí: 1. Los parientes en línea recta por consanguinidad o adopción. 2. Los colaterales por consanguinidad hasta el tercer grado. 3. Los condenados por haber tenido

participación en la muerte dolosa del cónyuge o persona con la que hubiera estado unida por análoga relación de afectividad a la conyugal.

Artículo 48: El Juez podrá dispensar, con justa causa y a instancia de parte, mediante resolución previa dictada en expediente de jurisdicción voluntaria, los impedimentos de muerte dolosa del cónyuge o persona con la que hubiera estado unida por análoga relación de afectividad a la conyugal y de parentesco de grado tercero entre colaterales. La dispensa ulterior convalida, desde su celebración, el matrimonio cuya nulidad no haya sido instada judicialmente por alguna de las partes.

Without prejudice to the responsibilities and rights acquired in good faith by third parties, registration of the marriage may take place at any time on presentation of the certificate of the pertinent details, as referred to above.

Article 7 of the CA with CIE has been amended by Law 15/2015, of 2 July 2015, on voluntary jurisdiction,

Ley 26/1992, de 10 de noviembre, por la que se aprueba el Acuerdo de Cooperación del Estado con la Islámica de España Comisión
Artículo 7.
1. Se atribuye efectos civiles al matrimonio celebrado según la forma religiosa establecida en la Ley Islámica, desde el momento de su celebración, si los contrayentes reúnen los requisitos de capacidad exigidos por el Código Civil.
Los contrayentes expresarán el consentimiento ante alguna de las personas expresadas en el número 1 del artículo 3 y, al menos, dos testigos mayores de edad.
Para el pleno reconocimiento de tales efectos, será necesaria la inscripción del matrimonio en el Registro Civil.
2. Las personas que deseen inscribir el matrimonio celebrado en la forma prevista en el número anterior, deberán acreditar previamente su capacidad matrimonial, mediante copia del acta o resolución previa expedida por el Secretario judicial, Notario, Encargado del Registro Civil o funcionario diplomático o consular Encargado del Registro Civil conforme a la Ley del Registro Civil y que deberá contener, en su caso, juicio acreditativo de la capacidad matrimonial. No podrá practicarse la inscripción si se hubiera celebrado el matrimonio transcurridos más de seis meses desde la fecha de dicha acta o desde la fecha de la resolución correspondiente.

3. Una vez celebrado el matrimonio, el representante de la Comunidad Islámica en que se hubiera contraído aquel extenderá certificación expresiva de la celebración del mismo, con los requisitos necesarios para su inscripción y las menciones de las circunstancias del expediente o acta previa que necesariamente incluirán el nombre y apellidos del Secretario judicial, Notario, Encargado del Registro Civil o funcionario diplomático o consular que la hubiera extendido, la fecha y número de protocolo en su caso. Esta certificación se remitirá por medios electrónicos, en la forma que reglamentariamente se determine, junto con la certificación acreditativa de la capacidad representante de la Comunidad Islámica para celebrar matrimonios, de conformidad con lo previsto en el apartado 1 del artículo 3, dentro del plazo de cinco días al Encargado del Registro Civil competente para su inscripción. Igualmente extenderá en las dos copias del acta o resolución previa de capacidad matrimonial diligencia expresiva de la celebración del matrimonio, entregando una a los contrayentes y conservará la otra como acta de la celebración en el archivo de la Comunidad.
4. Sin perjuicio de las responsabilidades a que haya lugar y de los derechos adquiridos de buena fe por terceras personas, la inscripción del matrimonio celebrado conforme al presente Acuerdo podrá ser promovida también en cualquier tiempo, mediante presentación de la certificación diligenciada a que se refiere el número anterior.
5. Las normas de este artículo relativas al procedimiento para hacer efectivo el derecho que en el mismo se establece, se ajustarán a las modificaciones que en el futuro se produzcan en la legislación del Registro Civil, previa audiencia de la Comisión Islámica de España.

12.2 Private International Law

According to the Civil Code, two Muslim foreigners can get married in accordance with the Spanish Civil Code or the personal law appropriate to either of them (article 50). In this last case (article 12.3 Civil Code) if the personal law of the foreigner is against public order (for example in the case of a foreign law that allows the marriage of children) would be an exception.

Código Civil español

Artículo 50: Si ambos contrayentes son extranjeros, podrá celebrarse el matrimonio en España con arreglo a la forma prescrita para los españoles

o cumpliendo la establecida por la ley personal de cualquiera de ellos.
Artículo 12.3: En ningún caso tendrá aplicación la ley extranjera cuando resulte contraria al orden público.

Spanish law does not grant legal validity to Islamic divorce. If those who have married in Spain want to divorce, they will have to proceed in accordance with the provisions of Spanish law regarding divorce.

CHAPTER 13

Criminal Law

The Criminal Code contains a limited number of specific provisions under chapter IV on felonies related to the exercise of fundamental public rights and liberties. Subchapter 2 is dedicated to "felonies against freedom of conscience, religious feelings and respect for the death". Among felonies that protect the free exercise of worship as guaranteed by article 16 of the Constitution, one article penalises those who force others to attend (or prevent them from attending) religious ceremonies. Another article refers to the interruption of religious ceremonies and perpetrating profane acts in a place of worship or at religious ceremonies. Finally, another article refers to publicly denigrating religious dogmas or their sacred objects or publicly insulting those who profess a religion or those who do not profess any religion whatsoever.

Any Muslim who is forced to practise acts of worship of Islam or another religion or who is prevented from participating in Islamic acts is protected by article 522 of the Penal Code, which also protects those who, by violent means, are forced to attend any act of worship, or to carry out acts that reveal whether they profess Islam or are forced to change the religion they profess. The punishment is a fine of from four to ten months (assessed on a monthly basis with reference to the defendant's means by the judge in each case).

Código Penal

Artículo 522: Incurrirán en la pena de multa de cuatro a diez meses:
1.º Los que, por medio de violencia, intimidación, fuerza o cualquier otro apremio ilegítimo impidan a un miembro o miembros de una confesión religiosa practicar los actos propios de las creencias que profesen, o asistir a los mismos.
2.º Los que por iguales medios fuercen a otro u otros a practicar o concurrir a actos de culto o ritos, o a realizar actos reveladores de profesar o no profesar una religión, o a mudar la que profesen.

The Penal Code also protects Muslim ceremonies from being violently interrupted by anyone.

Artículo 523: Quien por violencia, intimidación, tumultuosa o imposición impida, interrumpa o perturbe los actos, funciones, ceremonias o

> manifestaciones de confesiones religiosas inscritas en el correspondiente registro público del Ministerio de Justicia será sancionado con pena privativa de libertad de 6 meses a 6 años, si el hecho fue cometido en el lugar de culto, y con multa de 4 a 10 meses si se perpetra en otro lugar.

Mosques or other sacred placed are also protected by the Penal Code from acts of desecration if such acts that can undermine the religious feelings of Muslims have been performed with that intention (the intention must be proved). This attitude can be punished even with imprisonment from six months to 6 years.

> Artículo 524: El que, en templo, lugar destinado al culto o en ceremonias religiosas ejecutare actos de profanación en ofensa de los sentimientos religiosos legalmente tutelados será castigado con la pena de prisión de seis meses a un año o multa de 12 a 24 meses.

The crime of blasphemy no longer exists in the Spanish Penal Code. But some attitudes regarding the heavy mocking of sacred persons or dogmas could be considered as crimes when it is proved that the offender's aim is not just to criticise in terms accepted by freedom of speech, but the act constitutes "hate speech" (words uttered with the only aim of expressing hate). The constitutional court has repeatedly asserted that freedom of speech does not include a right to insult even though this freedom includes expressions that can offend, shock or disturb as long as they are uttered on an *animus criticandi* or *animus jocandi* basis but not from *animus injuriandi*. In other words, freedom of speech allows people to make jokes or to criticise other people or attitudes. But it does not protect those expressions uttered with the clear aim of humiliating others.[1]

In other words, hate speech regarding Islam or another religion occurs when a drawing or representation shown in public is expressed or uttered not with the intention of criticising or even making fun in the terms admitted by freedom of speech, but with the intention of offending religious feelings.

This same article also protects ideological feelings, in other words the feelings of those who are not religious believers and are attacked by hate speech because of their lack of religious belief. In those cases, the punishment laid down by the law is not prison, but just a fine assessed from eight to 12 months.

1 The dividing line between hate speech and freedom of speech is finally decided by Judges. There are some criteria laid down by our Constitutional Court: for example, if the controversial opinion is connected to veracious facts of public interests freedom of speech prevails over the other legal right or legal interest (respect of religious feelings). See Ferreiro (2014).

Artículo 525:
1. Quien, con el fin de ofender los sentimientos religiosos de los miembros de una confesión religiosa, menosprecie públicamente sus dogmas, creencias, ritos o ceremonia en público, verbalmente o por escrito o insulte, también públicamente, a quienes los profesen o practiquen, deberá incurrir en el castigo de una multa de ocho a doce meses.
2. En las mismas penas incurrirán los que menosprecien públicamente, verbalmente o por escrito, a los que no profesen ni crean religión alguna.

Finally, the Criminal Code also criminalises the desecration of tombs or sepulchres. This article protects, more than religious freedom or religious feelings, the "due respect for the memory of the dead".

Artículo 526: Será sancionado quien, sin el debido respeto a la memoria de los muertos, rompa tumbas o sepulturas, profanare un cadáver o sus cenizas o, con el fin de ultrajar, destruya, altere o dañe las urnas, panteones, lápidas o nichos funerarios, será sancionado. con pena de prisión de tres a cinco meses o multa de seis a diez meses.

CHAPTER 14

Islamic Dress

Religious freedom is established in article 16.1 of the Spanish Constitution which guarantees the freedom of ideology, religion and worship of individuals and communities, with no restrictions on their expression other than any that may be necessary to maintain public order as protected by law. The Religious Freedom Act implements this fundamental right. Article 2 of LOLR refers to several manifestations of the religious freedom of individuals. One of them is the right of every person to express their own religious beliefs freely. And any person can freely express their own creed not only orally, but also by action. This manifestation of religious freedom, as the European Court of Human Rights has proclaimed,[1] includes the right to dress according to one's religion.

Obviously, all manifestations of human rights (such as religious freedom) have limitations. The Constitution mentions those "necessary to maintain public order as protected by law". The Religious Freedom Act implements two of these mentioned limitations: the fundamental rights of others and public order which is like a triangular concept formed by three aspects: public safety, public health and public morality.[2] There are no specific regulations on religious dress, but with the existing regulation we can say in general terms than wearing a *hjjab* or any other Islamic dress is perfectly legal if this attitude does not undermine the human rights of others or any specific aspects of the public order: public safety, health and morality.

14.1 Hijab and Identity

Sometimes the guarantee of public safety requires the authorities to adopt preventive measures such as the identification of people. In this sense, the use of religious symbols has presented some problems in relation to their use in mandatory photographs in identification documents such as National Identity Documents (DNI) and Passports.

1 X v. Reino Unido, decision on the admissibility of application n. 7992/77, 12 July 1978 (in "Decision & Reports" 14, pp. 234–235). The plaintiff was a Sikh resident in the United Kingdom, who had been issued with repeated traffic tickets for refusing to comply with the rule that required motorcycle riders to use mandatory protective helmets. See Martinez-Torrón (2009).

2 LOLR article 3.1 See chapter 1.1.1.

Royal Decree 1553/2005, which regulates the issue of the national identity card, requires (article 5.1) a photograph "with the head totally uncovered", but adds, "and without dark glasses or any other garment that could prevent or hinder the identification of the person". For some time, the Ministry of the Interior interpreted the obligation to take the photograph "with the head totally uncovered" in a way that accords with religious freedom, that is, admitting as an exception the possibility of wearing religious symbols as long as they do not prevent the perfect identification of the person.

Regarding the issuing of passports, Royal Decree 896/2003, when referring to the necessary photography (article 4), does not refer to having the head completely uncovered, but simply prohibits the wearing of dark glasses "or any other garment that prevents the identification of the person". Therefore, it is possible to wear a *hijab* in a passport photograph if it does not prevent the identification of the person. On 21 August 2008, the General Director of the Police and the Civil Guard issued a report that permitted photographs in which the applicant has their head covered with a scarf, headdress or garment imposed by a religion if "the oval of the face appears totally uncovered from the hairline to the chin, so that it does not impede or make it difficult to identify the person". Eventually, the decision whether the *hijab* does or does not prevent the identification of the person rests with the judges.

14.2 Hijab in Schools

The first controversy over the use of the hijab in school arose in 2002 when a girl was not allowed to enter a private school funded by the State (*concertado*) in San Lorenzo del Escorial (Madrid) with a *hijab* on her head. Two other cases followed in 2007, in Girona and in Ceuta. In these three cases the education authorities ordered the girls' readmission, arguing that the right to receive education prevailed over the schools' internal regulations on clothing. The most significant case that defeated this logic occurred in 2010 at a school in Pozuelo de Alarcón (Madrid) where a 16-year-old girl was not allowed in school because she was wearing a *hijab*. Because he upheld in an official report the girl's right to wear the hijab as a legal manifestation of religious freedom, the deputy director of the Ministry of Justice (who is in fact the author of this section) was then ceased from his post at the Ministry.[3] The Superior Court of Justice of Madrid

3 Juan Ferreiro was deputy director of the Ministry of Justice from 2006 to 2010. See https://elpais.com/diario/2010/05/11/sociedad/1273528803_850215.html, accessed 13 May 2010.

considered that the school's internal rules, an expression of its legal autonomy,[4] prevailed over the girl's religious freedom.[5] Unfortunately, due to lack of legal assistance, the girl's family did not appeal this resolution before the Supreme Court.

Because, although the LOLR indicates that public security is a limitation on religious freedom,[6] and law can be interpreted as a part of public security, in Spain, unlike in France, no law has been passed that prohibits students from wearing ostentatious religious symbols at public schools. Of course, the Spanish Religious Freedom Act could be amended to include that limitation, as did the French Law of 2004 (Law 2004–228 of 15 March). But, in any case, this amendment should have been done, not by bylaws or other inferior norms as has happened in some state schools, but in the Spanish Parliament by means of not a regular law but an "organic law", the only type that, according to our Constitution (article 81.1), can regulate (or modify) fundamental rights.

Constitución Española 1978

Artículo 81.1: Son leyes orgánicas las relativas al desarrollo de los derechos fundamentales y de las libertades públicas, las que aprueben los Estatutos de Autonomía y el régimen electoral general y las demás previstas en la Constitución

Introducing additional limitations to a fundamental right (in this case religious freedom) by means of inferior norms (such as the internal rules of a state or public school) is simply unconstitutional because it violates the principle of legal hierarchy (article 9.3 CE) and the constitutional mandate that states that fundamental rights must be regulated by organic laws.

Artículo 9. 3. La Constitución garantiza el principio de legalidad, la jerarquía normativa, [...].

4 Ley Orgánica de Educación 2/2006, de 29 de diciembre. Art 120: 2. Los centros docentes dispondrán de autonomía para elaborar, aprobar y ejecutar un proyecto educativo y un proyecto de gestión, así como las normas de organización y funcionamiento del centro.

5 Judgment 129/2013, of 8 February.

6 LOLR article 3.1. See chapter 1.1.1.

14.3 Bans on Niqab and Burka

This issue was raised for the first time in the city of Lleida (Catalonia) where a municipal regulation prohibited the use of the burqa in public spaces. Despite the virtual non-existence of this garment in Spain, several municipalities, mainly in Catalonia, followed Lleida's footsteps.[7] A Muslim association in Lleida appealed Lleida city council's rule to the courts.

The Supreme Court, in a ruling of 14 February 2013, annulled that local regulation. It argued that in the absence of a national law prohibiting the burqa the municipalities had no competence to regulate central aspects of fundamental rights (a competence reserved by article 53 of the CE to the law), such as the right of a woman to dress according to her religious beliefs. The Court added that it was not correct to suppose that a woman who wears a burqa acts under pressure. And, if so, the woman can always count on the protection of the law and of the public powers themselves. Regarding the limits of religious freedom established expressly by the Religious Freedom Act (fundamental rights of others and public order), the Court states that wearing a headscarf does not undermine either the fundamental rights of others or public order, because according to the Spanish Public Security Act whenever it is necessary on public security grounds anyone can be required to reveal their face to be identified.

Ley Orgánica 4/2015, de 30 de marzo, de protección de la seguridad ciudadana.
BOE núm. 77, de 31/03/2015

Artículo 16. "Identificación de personas. 1. En el cumplimiento de sus funciones de indagación y prevención delictiva, así como para la sanción de infracciones penales y administrativas, los agentes de las Fuerzas y Cuerpos de Seguridad podrán requerir la identificación de las personas [...] incluida la identificación de las personas cuyo rostro no sea visible total o parcialmente por utilizar cualquier tipo de prenda u objeto que lo cubra, impidiendo o dificultando la identificación [...]. En la práctica de la identificación se respetarán estrictamente los principios de proporcionalidad, igualdad de trato y no discriminación [...]".

7 https://elpais.com/diario/2010/06/18/opinion/1276812004_850215.html, accessed 26 June 2010.

After the controversies over the prohibition of the full veil, there has been no further controversy over the use of the *hijab*, which has become a usual garment for many Muslim women of different ages. There is still no regulation that prohibits its use in public spaces or in the workplace. But that does not, as repeatedly reported by Islamic entities, prevent there being numerous cases of Muslim women who are not hired because they wear *hijab*.

Bibliography

Astor, Avi, *Rebuilding Islam in Contemporary Spain. The Politics of Mosque Establishment, 1976–2013* (Brighton: Sussex Academic Press, 2017).

Cano, Isabel, "El uso del velo islámico en el ámbito educativo", in Rodríguez Blanco, Miguel (coord.), *El velo islámico y los derechos fundamentales de la mujer* (Madrid: Canis Majoris, 2020), pp. 91–127.

Cembrero, Ignacio, *La España de Alá* (Madrid: La Esfera de los Libros, 2016).

Ciáurriz, María José, "La asistencia religiosa en los centros públicos", in Motilla, Agustín (ed.), *Los musulmanes en España. Libertad religiosa e identidad cultural.* (Madrid: Trotta, 2004), pp. 137–165.

Contreras Mazario, José Maria, *¿Hacia un islam español? Un estudio de derecho y política* (Valencia: Tirant Humanidades, 2017).

Corpas Aguirre, Maria de los Ángeles, *Las comunidades islámicas en la España actual (1960–2008)* (Madrid: Universidad Nacional de Educación a Distancia, 2010).

De la Cueva, Julio, Hernando de Larramendi, Miguel and Planet, Ana I. (eds.), *Encrucijadas del cambio religioso en España: secularización, cristianismo e islam.* (Granada: Comares, 2018).

Díez de Velasco, Francisco, *Religiones en España. Historia y presente* (Madrid: Editorial Akal, 2012).

Fernández-Coronado, Ana, *Estado y confesiones religiosas: un nuevo modelo de relación (los pactos con las confesiones: leyes 24, 25 y 26 de 1992)* (Madrid: Civitas, 1995).

Ferreiro, Juan, *Relaciones Iglesia-Estado en la II República Española* (Barcelona: Ediciones Atelier, 2005).

Ferreiro, Juan, "Los órganos de la Administración española encargados de la relación jurídico-técnica con la Santa Sede: la Dirección General de Asuntos Religiosos y la Subdirección de relaciones con la Santa Sede", in Vázquez, José María, Rodríguez Blanco, Miguel and Salido López, Mercedes (dirs.), *Iglesia Católica y Relaciones Internacionales* (Granada: Comares, 2008), pp. 280–291.

Ferreiro, Juan, "Símbolos religiosos en la escuela pública: crucifijos en el aula y alumnas con *hiyab*" in *Educación y Libertad* (Madrid: Dykinson, 2012), pp. 81–126.

Ferreiro, Juan, "Training Centres for Imams in Spain", in Aslan, Ednan and Windisch, Zsófia (eds.), *The Training of Imams and Teachers for Islamic Education in Europe.* (Frankfurt am Main: Peter Lang, 2012), pp. 257–272.

Ferreiro, Juan, "Libertad de expresión y sensibilidad religiosa: estudio legislativo y jurisprudencial" in *Revista Española de Derecho Canónico y Derecho Eclesiástico del Estado*, 34 (2014).

Ferreiro, Juan, "Islamic education in Spain" in Aslan, Ednan and Hermansen, Marcia (eds.) *Islam and citizenship Education* (Wiesbaden: Springer, 2015), pp. 123–137.

Ferreiro, Juan, "Desarrollo de los Acuerdos de Cooperación de 1992: luces y sombras", in *Revista General de Derecho Canónico y Derecho Eclesiástico del Estado*, 44 (2017).

Ferreiro, Juan, "Teaching religion in Public Schools in Spain. The Constitutional Principle of Cooperation makes the difference" in Aslan, Ednan and Rausch, Margaret (eds.) *Religious Education. Between Radicalism and Tolerance* (Wiesbaden: Springer, 2018), pp. 93–113.

Ferreiro, Juan, "Imam training in the legal context of islam in Spain", in Hashas, Mohammed, de Ruiter, Jan Jaap and Vinding, Niels Valdemar (eds.), *Imams in Western Europe: Developments, Transformations, and Institutional Challenges* (Amsterdam: Amsterdam University Press, 2018), pp. 337–357.

Ferreiro, Juan, "El derecho a portar símbolos religiosos como manifestación de la libertad religiosa" in *El velo islámico y los derechos fundamentales de la mujer* (Madrid: Canis Majoris, 2020), pp. 41–90.

Ferreiro, Juan (ed.), *Islam and State in the European Union: Church-State Relationships, Reality of Islam, Imams Training Centres.* (Frankfurt am Main: Peter Lang, 2011).

Guia, Aitana, *The Muslim struggle for Civil Rights in Spain. Promoting Democracry Through Migrant Engagement, 1985–2010* (Brighton: Sussex Academic Press, 2014).

Lorenzo, Paula-Peña, María Teresa, "La enseñanza religiosa islámica", in Motilla, Agustín (ed.), *Los musulmanes en España. Libertad religiosa e identidad cultural.* (Madrid: Editorial Trotta, 2004), pp. 249–279.

Mantecón Sancho, Joaquín, "Los nuevos estatutos de la CIE, una solución interlocutoria", in *Revista General de Derecho Canónico y Derecho Eclesiástico del Estado*, 40 (2016).

Martínez-Torrón, Javier, "Los límites a la libertad de religión y de creencia en el Convenio Europeo de Derechos Humanos", in *Revista General de Derecho Canónico y Derecho Eclesiástico del Estado*, 2 (2003).

Martínez-Torrón, Javier, "La cuestión del velo islámico en la jurisprudencia de Estrasburgo", in *Derecho y Religión*, 4 (2009): 87–109.

Martínez-Torrón, Javier, "COVID-19 y libertad religiosa: ¿problemas nuevos o soluciones antiguas", in *COVID-19 y libertad religiosa* Iustel (2020): 23–32

Ministerio de Justicia, *Informe anual sobre la situación de la libertad religiosa en España 2018* ("El derecho a recibir sepultura digna sin discriminación por motivos religiosos") (Madrid: Ministerio de Justicia, 2019).

Moreras, Jordi, "Muslims in Spain: between the Historical Heritage and the Minority Construction", in *The Muslim World*, vol. 92 (2002): 129–142.

Moreras, Jordi, *Els imams de Catalunya* (Barcelona: Editorial Empúries, 2007).

Moreras, Jordi, *Garantes de la tradición. Viejos y nuevos roles en el ejercicio de la autoridad religiosa islámica en contexto migratorio. El caso de Cataluña.* (Universitat Rovira i Virgili. Doctoral dissertation, 2009).

Moreras, Jordi, *Una mesquita al barri: conflicte, espai públic i integració urbana dels oratoris musulmans a Catalunya.* (Barcelona: Fundació Jaume Bofill, 2009).

Moreras, Jordi, "Spain", in Egdunas Racius-Stephanie Müssig (eds.), *Yearbook of Muslims in Europe.* Volume 12 (Leiden: Brill, 2021), pp. 616–629.

Moreras, Jordi-Solé, Ariadna, "Genealogies of death. A comparison between the Moroccan and Senegalese funerary rituals in diaspora", in Koskinen-Koivisto, Eerika, Saramo, Samira and Snellman, Hanna (eds.), *Transnational Death* (Helsinki: Finnish Literature Society (Studia Fennica Ethnologia Series), 2019), pp. 118–135.

Moreras, Jordi-Tarrés, Sol, *Guía para la gestión de la diversidad religiosa en cementerios y Servicios funerarios.* (Madrid: Observatorio del Pluralismo Religioso en España-Fundación Pluralismo y Convivencia, 2013a).

Moreras, Jordi-Tarrés, Sol, "Topografía de la otra muerte. Los cementerios musulmanes en España (siglos XX–XXI)", in Caerols, José J. (ed.), *Religio in labyrintho,* (Madrid: Sociedad Española de Ciencias de las Religiones-Escolar y Mayo Editores, 2013b), pp. 309–321.

Motilla, Agustín (ed.), *Los musulmanes en España. Libertad religiosa e identidad cultural* (Madrid: Editorial Trotta, 2004).

Pelayo, Daniel, *Las comunidades ideológicas y religiosas, la personalidad jurídica y la actividad registral* (Madrid: Ministerio de Justicia, 2007).

Pérez-Agote, Alfonso, *Cambio religioso en España. Los avatares de la secularización* (Madrid: Centro de Investigaciones Sociológicas, 2012).

Planet Contreras, Ana I. (ed.), *Observing Islam in Spain. Contemporary Politics and Social Dynamics* (Leiden: Brill, 2018).

Ramírez Navalón, Rosa Maria, "Las festividades religiosas", in *Acuerdos del estado español con los judíos, musulmanes y protestantes* (Salamanca: Universidad Pontificia de Salamanca, 1994), pp. 249–254.

Rodrigo Lara, Belén, "La libertad religiosa en España durante la pandemia del COVID-19", in *COVID-19 y libertad religiosa* Iustel (2009): 130–134.

Rodríguez Blanco, Miguel, *Libertad religiosa y confesiones. El régimen jurídico de los lugares de culto.* (Madrid: Centro de Estudios Políticos y Constitucionales, 2000).

Rodríguez Blanco, Miguel, "Asistencia religiosa penitenciaria de las confesiones minoritarias con Acuerdo de cooperación", in Martín Sánchez, Isidoro and González Sánchez, Marcos (coord.), *Algunas cuestiones controvertidas del ejercicio del derecho fundamental de libertad religiosa en España* (Madrid: Fundación Universitaria Española, 2009), pp. 183–207.

Rosón, Javier-Tarrés, Sol-Moreras, Jordi, "Islamic religious education in Spain", in Alvarez Veinguer, A., Dietz, G., Jozsa, D.P. and Knauth, T. (eds), *Islam in Education in European Countries: Pedagogical Concepts and Empirical Findings* (Münster/New York: Waxmann, 2009).

Tarrés, Sol-Rosón, Javier, "¿Musulmanes o inmigrantes? La institucionalización del islam en España (1860–1992)", in *Revista CIDOB d'Afers Internacionals* 115 (2017): 165–168.

Index

Printed in the United States
by Baker & Taylor Publisher Services